TENNESSEE HERO
CONFEDERATE BRIGADIER
GENERAL JOHN ADAMS

TENNESSEE HERO
CONFEDERATE BRIGADIER
GENERAL JOHN ADAMS

BRYAN W. LANE

Foreword by Eric A. Jacobson, CEO, Battle of Franklin Trust

THE History PRESS

Published by The History Press
Charleston, SC
www.historypress.net

Front cover, bottom, image courtesy of the Library of Congress.
Opposite photo in author's possession.

First published 2017

Manufactured in the United States

ISBN 9781625859167

Library of Congress Control Number: 2017938347

Notice: The information in this book is true and complete to the best of our knowledge. It is offered without guarantee on the part of the author or The History Press. The author and The History Press disclaim all liability in connection with the use of this book.

To John and Brent, and all who hear the past whisper

Contents

Foreword

Nearly three decades ago, when I was first reading about the Battle of Franklin, I learned who Brigadier General John Adams was. Ever since then, the story of his life, and his death, has been of interest to me. I remain convinced that Adams's death was a singular event of the battle and one that remained seared in the minds of those who saw it. It also became part of American Civil War legend. But as the years passed, I learned that his personal life was just as fascinating. From his Tennessee roots to his long career in the U.S. Army and even being stationed in Minnesota, where I was born and raised, there was a unique nature to Adams's story. Then there was his family. His wife, Georgiana, was strength personified. She raised their children after the war, largely by herself, and her dedication to his memory never wavered.

For over a decade there has been a movement to reclaim important portions of the Franklin battlefield, a battlefield that most people considered lost. Nearly two hundred acres have been saved just since 2005. At the same time, there has been a wider telling of Franklin's story to a growing number of people. Many of those same people are hearing and reading about John Adams for the first time. They learn how a man, a husband and father, a soldier, astride his trusted horse, came charging through the smoke of battle and led his troops onto the pages of history.

Tennessee Hero is one of those books that should have been written years ago, but luckily for us it was not. Instead, in this book Bryan Lane gives John

Adams the treatment that his life and his military career deserve. Those of us who understand the importance of the Civil War, and those of us in Franklin, owe Bryan a debt of gratitude for taking on this important subject.

ERIC JACOBSON

Preface

Thomas Gibson was Brigadier General John Adams's cousin. Gibson grew up in Nashville, Tennessee, and during the Civil War he served on General Adams's staff along with the General's brother, Thomas Patton Adams. When Thomas Patton Adams died in 1901, Gibson wrote to his widow, Mary Elizabeth Bragg Adams, to express his condolences. The letter to "Cousin Mollie" ended with these words:

> *I meet so many persons particularly young people who know so little about the commands that their kin people belonged to and campaigns and battles they were in that it makes me feel like we probably have been too careless about informing them. In after years they will then want or might want information that would be pleasant to know and of advantage to them.*[1]

Over the years, Thomas Gibson did what he could to share and, in some cases, correct information about those battles and campaigns. In May 1907, he presented a collection of General John Adams's items to the Tennessee Historical Society in Nashville, Tennessee. The General's widow, Georgiana McDougall Adams, had given the relics to Gibson shortly before her death and requested the items be donated to the society. The collection included one of the General's frock coats, his red sash, his saddle, a flag that had been presented to one of his regiments during the war and several other possessions and documents, including a prized letter from Confederate major general William Wing Loring. (Unfortunately, the whereabouts of the Loring letter is unknown today.) What was not included were letters, papers or diaries of the General.[2] To this day, we do not know if any of his writings, other than a few letters in California and a couple written to the United States Military Academy, exist and, if they do, where they are. So this biography is the story of his life, pieced together from his writings where they are available, the recollections of his peers and other records.

Acknowledgements

Many people helped me over the years. I want to thank my friend Randy Duncan, who was editor, critic, encourager and also supplied excellent photographs for this book. I also would like to recognize and thank my sister, Beth DeHahn. In the beginning, she played a key role in getting important information about General Adams and over the years helped with editing. Marsha Smith is an extraordinary researcher and furnished many important and interesting details. Dolores Greenwald, Leesa Harman, Margaret Brown and Suzanne Sparks of the Williamson County Public Library in Franklin, Tennessee, shared their time and skills and were a great help on this project. Thomas Cartwright, the great historian and storyteller, worked at the Carter House when I first met him many years ago. He graciously supplied information about John Adams. Thomas is at the Lotz House now and still giving wonderful tours. David Fraley, formerly of the Lotz House and Carter House, shared his time and knowledge generously. David and I spent a rainy afternoon together walking the final steps of the General, from the Collins Farm, up the Lewisburg Pike and finally to the spot near where he would have fallen.

I would like to thank Eric Jacobson of the Battle of Franklin Trust for his encouragement over the years. Rob DeHart of the Tennessee State Museum helped by supplying pictures of General Adams's items that are in the possession of the museum in Nashville. Will Gorenfeld supplied terrific information regarding the dragoon years. John Rhodehamel of the Huntington Library in California sent me copies of the Adams letters from the Cave Couts collection. Christopher Nordmann of St. Louis provided me with information on Georgiana and the children. Keith Arnold of Fort Crook sent me dispatches. Judith Sibley, Suzanne Christoff and Louise Friend all were so kind to send me what they had regarding John Adams's time at the United States Military Academy and Carlisle Barracks.

Elizabeth White, of the Giles County Historical Society, shared an afternoon of her time with me, and we looked through documents that the General had actually touched and signed. That was a thrill, and I will never forget looking at those papers. Special thanks to the Adams family branch that befriended and "adopted" me as a cousin: Jeanne Crawford, Rosalie Adams Cox, Rita Grace Adams, Larry Adams and Patton Adams, all of whom generously shared details about the General.

Jim Huffman, Dan Speer, Ronnie Clemmons, Tim Burgess, Gary Swanson, Carolyn Edmondson and others whom I cannot now recall all shared what they had so that General Adams might be remembered.

Thank you to Jaclyn Lyons, Hilary Parrish and the other good people at Arcadia Publishing and The History Press who believed in this story and published this book.

And last, but not least, my wife, Connie, who has been with me from the beginning on this—thank you, dear.

Chapter 1

"The Grandest Performance of the War"

Thursday, December 1, 1881

The war was over now and the dead long buried, yet on this night the familiar dead seemed to live again in the minds and stories of the old soldiers who had gathered at the Masonic temple in Louisville, Kentucky, for a banquet being held by the Louisville Southern Historical Society. Former Tennessee governor James Davis Porter accompanied his friend, former Confederate major general Benjamin Franklin "Frank" Cheatham, to Louisville, where Cheatham would deliver his paper on the "Incident at Spring Hill" and talk about the terrible Battle of Franklin that followed.

In the audience that evening were former foes, men from the North and South, but there was no hint of animosity. They enjoyed a fine meal and then listened together as the general made his presentation. Governor Porter had firsthand knowledge of the events of the late war because he had been a member of Cheatham's staff. He listened intently to his friend's presentation and relived those tragic hours when so much hung in the balance and so many lives were at stake.

After the speech, clusters of aging men gathered and talked in quiet tones of things they had seen and done. Several former Federal soldiers approached Cheatham's table. One of the men had commanded a Federal regiment at Franklin, at the point of the line where General John Adams fell. The former officer introduced himself to the southern gentlemen and then made this request: "Tell us something of the personal history of John Adams." Governor Porter told the northern men what he knew of Adams. After Porter finished, the former Federal officer reflected for a moment and stated, "His conduct at Franklin was the grandest performance of the war."[3]

Chapter 2

Nashville

John Adams's paternal grandparents, Nathan and Martha Patton Adams, came to this country from Strabane, County Tyrone, in what is today Northern Ireland. That is the Ulster province, and the inhabitants of that region would come to be known as "Scots-Irish" because many had migrated there from the Scottish Borders region during the reign of English King James I.[4] The Scots-Irish were mostly Protestant and Presbyterian. Many of their Irish neighbors were Catholic. England's Test Act enforced the authority of the Church of England. These religious conflicts, added to economic woes brought about by high taxes levied by the English, led many from this area to migrate to what would become the United States. Nathan and Martha Adams decided to leave their home in Strabane and make their way in the New World. Martha Patton was only sixteen when she married Nathan Adams, and the newlyweds packed their things, said goodbye to family and friends, left the Emerald Isle and sailed to New York not long after their wedding in 1784.[5]

Voyages in those days were more often than not grueling ordeals. There was overcrowding and sickness, horrible smells, bad food and water and foul air, and the journeys lasted several weeks. The newlyweds survived the crossing and made it to their destination, arriving in New York City, where they stayed for three years. There is no record to indicate why, but they decided to return to Ireland, where they started a family. One of their children, Thomas Patton Adams (John Adams's father), was born in Ireland on March 1, 1796. Nathan and Martha and their children moved back to the United States in 1811, and this time it was for good. On this second and final crossing, the Adamses sailed aboard a ship called *Prosperity*, and their belongings were put on another vessel. *Prosperity* made it to port. The other ship, with all their possessions, sank.[6] Fortunately, when they landed in New York, Nathan's brother John had already established himself in the banking industry. The future General John Adams's namesake had immigrated to this country in 1794. John Adams, the elder, was very successful and eventually became president of the Fulton Bank in New York City and treasurer of the New York Hospital and also the American Bible Society. He would have been able to provide his relatives with a place to stay until they could make it on their own.[7]

The new country was about making your own way, and to that end Nathan, Martha and their children left New York City and moved to Philadelphia, Pennsylvania. Once there, Nathan earned a living as a storekeeper on North Second Street. His name first appears on a registry in that city as of January 1, 1813.[8] They might have stayed there, but Nathan died in January 1817, leaving behind Martha and their eleven children.[9] The recently widowed Mrs. Adams did not tarry in Philadelphia. The following year, she and the children who were still at home moved out west to Nashville, Tennessee, eight hundred miles away. She chose Nashville because one of her daughters, Margaret, had married a prominent Nashville businessman, George Crockett Sr. Another daughter, Jane, would later marry Nashvillian Robert Gibson (cousin Thomas Gibson's parents).[10]

An Adams family history indicates that Robert and Jane Adams Gibson lived across the road from Andrew Jackson. Martha and her children lived with the Gibsons until she could buy her own home.[11] (Mr. Gibson had known his future brother-in-law Thomas Patton Adams when they lived in Ireland. The two also lived at the same residence in Philadelphia, where Gibson offered Thomas Patton a job in Nashville, working for Crockett and Adams, a store that sold dry goods and groceries, everything from rope to linseed oil to whiskey.)[12]

John Adams's grandmother Martha Adams lived to be eighty-six and spent all the rest of her life in Nashville. Andrew Jackson became a family friend, and the Adams family story goes that Jackson never left Nashville for Washington without first stopping in to say goodbye to Martha.[13] We do know that Jackson knew Martha and others in that extended family because there are receipts that show the future president purchased items from Crockett and Adams.[14] When Martha Adams died, her pastor wrote a eulogy that described her as a "Christian, in all that is implied in a title

John Adams's parents, Thomas Patton Adams and Anne Tennant Adams. *Photo in author's possession.*

so expressive and endearing." The pastor also recalled "her placid brow at church, her happy smile at home, her gentle manners, and her affectionate tones of endearing kindness."[15]

John Adams's mother, Anne Tennant, came from Dumfries, Scotland, with her parents, Christopher and Isabella Stothard Tennant, in 1808.[16] Dumfries is in the southwestern part of Scotland, and Anne Tennant's hometown is actually only about two hundred miles distant from Strabane, Ireland, where Thomas Patton Adams was born. Of course, they were separated by the Irish Sea and likely would never have met had they not both come to this country. Anne was nine years old at the time of the voyage to America. Her birth date was the same as her future husband's: March 1. Unlike her future husband, Anne had only one sibling, a brother named Joseph. The Tennants first settled in Philadelphia, where they lived with Anne's uncle William Stothard. Anne Tennant later visited William's brother Robert Stothard in Nashville.[17] There she met a handsome young Irishman, and on Thursday, November 18, 1819,[18] Anne Tennant and Thomas Patton Adams were married by the Presbyterian minister William Hume. Thomas Patton was twenty-three and Anne was twenty.[19]

Right: "Old Hickory," Andrew Jackson. The Marquis de Lafayette made a special trip to meet Adams's family friend. *Library of Congress*.

Below: This post–Civil War picture of the Nashville waterfront gives an idea of the hustle and bustle of a busy river town. *Library of Congress*.

At the time of their marriage, Thomas and Anne lived in a town that had yet to gain the prominence it would later enjoy, but that would change quickly. Located on the Cumberland River and near the Natchez Trace, Nashville was founded in December 1779 when, after a long overland march, James Robertson and nine other men reached the area. Those first settlers were joined a few months later by a second party headed by John Donelson, who had traveled by boat. Donelson's contingent included his daughter Rachel, who would one day marry Andrew Jackson.[20] The group struggled to build a home in the wilderness. Their hard work paid off and blazed a trail for others who followed. After the War of 1812, lands formerly held by Native American tribes opened up for settlement in Alabama and Tennessee. The new settlers brought new skills, and the little settlement continued to grow. The first steamboat arrived in Nashville in 1818, and not long after that, the town became a marketplace for tobacco and cotton.[21] Warehouses sprang up along the riverfront, and it was not uncommon to see lines of wagons full of tobacco or cotton and later grain stretching for a half mile, waiting their turn to be unloaded.[22] Thomas Patton Adams accepted his brother-in-law's offer and went to work for Crockett and Adams. The growing need for goods and the arrival of steamboat traffic helped his employer prosper. Timing is everything, and his was very good, as his arrival and marriage seemed to coincide with the growing importance of his adopted home.

In 1823, the city had a population of 3,460 people, and in 1826, the state legislature began meeting there. On May 4, 1825, Nashville hosted a visit by the Revolutionary War hero the Marquis de Lafayette.[23] Arguably the most famous Nashvillian at the time of Lafayette's visit was the hero of the Battle of New Orleans, renowned Indian fighter and Adams family friend Andrew Jackson. When Jackson learned of Lafayette's arrival in this country, he sent the famous Frenchman a letter expressing his admiration. Lafayette, thrilled to receive a letter from "Old Hickory," replied, "I will not leave the United States before I have seeked [*sic*] and found the opportunity to express in person my high regard and sincere friendship." Lafayette came to Nashville, and his new friend was there to meet him and show him around the city.[24]

Joyous crowds greeted them everywhere they went. Jackson hosted a party at the Nashville Inn for Lafayette and some of Jackson's closest friends and supporters.[25] Although no records confirm this, it is possible that one of the folks in attendance at the party was young Thomas Patton Adams. The erstwhile Irishman, now a flourishing businessman, was making prominent friends in his adopted hometown.

Chapter 3

Adams to Pulaski

Less than six weeks after the visit of the Marquis, John Adams was born. The Adamses' fourth child arrived on Friday, July 1, 1825. The following day, the *Nashville Whig* ran an advertisement seeking a teacher for the Wertemberg Academy in Pulaski, Tennessee. The ad said the school was located on a prominence just outside town. The newspaper also contained a story about a local performance of a new song that featured a beautiful, haunting melody, entitled "Home, Sweet Home."[26]

The growing family lived on Summer Street (today's Fifth Avenue) in Nashville at the time of John Adams's birth, not far from the hustle and bustle of the docks along the Cumberland River and the downtown markets and shops. Less than a year after baby John's birth, Thomas Patton Adams moved the family a few blocks west, away from the river, to Spruce Street (today's Eighth Avenue).[27] Thomas's mother, Martha, bought a lot nearby.[28] John had two older brothers, Nathan and William Stothard. The family would grow to include Martha, Anne Tennant, George Crockett and Thomas Patton. Three other little boys did not make it out of childhood.[29]

There are no records of those days in the Adams household to indicate who did what, when. All we have are numbers in census books and deed books. We do know that Nathan would go on to become a lawyer and, according to his brothers and sisters, was rather tight-fisted with his money. He likely would have been a serious child. William Stothard Adams would become a banker in Memphis and be known to friends and acquaintances as "Uncle Billy." He joined Mississippi state troops during the Civil War.[30] George Crockett, who went by Crockett, moved to Memphis and clerked there but moved back to Pulaski, where he died while still a young man.[31] Martha married a lawyer named Thomas Eldridge and moved to Memphis. Anne did not marry and was probably the family caregiver, a role she continued even after the Civil War. The last of the children, Thomas Patton Adams, moved to Arlington, Tennessee, just east of Memphis. There he married a "beautiful and cultured woman," Mary Elizabeth Bragg, raised eight children and became successful in the cotton business.[32] And as for John, we know from his years at West Point that he could get into trouble, liked friends and social activities and liked to have fun.

Thomas Patton Adams is listed as a manager of this party, along with William H. Wharton, John Austin Wharton's father. *Courtesy of the Tennessee State Museum.*

As his family grew, so did Thomas Patton Adams's circle of friends and business acquaintances. In December 1828, Thomas Patton Adams was a "manager" of a party that was to be hosted for Andrew Jackson in Nashville. This was "In Honor of the Election of our distinguished fellow-citizen General Andrew Jackson to the presidency of the United States." There were several prominent members of Nashville society listed as managers on the flyer.[33] One of those was a young lawyer named William Harris Wharton, who, along with his brother John, grew up in Nashville. William Wharton would go on to become a founding father of the Texas Republic.[34] Wharton's son, John Austin Wharton, would one day cross paths with John Adams, and the result would be the worst episode of Adams's military career. However, that was all in the future, and in December 1828, Thomas Adams was looking forward to the ball that was set for Tuesday, December 23.[35] The city prepared to honor its great hero.

But the reception never took place. Earlier that month, President-elect Jackson's wife, Rachel, went into Nashville to buy new clothes. She would soon be first lady and needed to look the part. After shopping, she decided to stop in at the office of a friend who was the editor of the local newspaper.

While she was waiting for her friend to see her, she happened to pick up and read a campaign pamphlet that had been written to defend her and her husband, Andrew. There, once again, she saw accusations that had been leveled against the couple, including adultery and bigamy. (Her first husband failed to follow through on a planned divorce so she was, in the eyes of her detractors anyway, still married to him.) Reading these awful charges, she broke down, slumped over in a corner and began crying inconsolably. After several minutes, she managed to recover enough to get up off the floor, pull herself together and go home to the Hermitage, but she never truly recovered from that incident. On December 18, she caught a cold. Later, she felt a sharp pain in her chest and left arm and cried out. Andrew rushed to her side and summoned doctors. They did their best, but they could not save Rachel, and on Sunday, December 22, the day before the planned reception, she died. A newspaper article had predicted before the tragic loss of his beloved wife that the party would be filled with "hilarity and joy." Now there was only grief. On December 24, church bells tolled from 1:00 to 2:00 p.m., the hour of her funeral.[36]

Jackson did ascend to the office of president of the United States. During his administration, the country added roads, including a military road in southern middle Tennessee that John Adams would travel on his final journey into the state. President Jackson also forced the removal of Native Americans from their homeland with the Indian Removal Act. The path the Native Americans took to their new "home" would forever after be known as the "Trail of Tears." He also vetoed a rechartering of the Bank of the United States. That led to the creation of state banks. One of the new banks created in Tennessee was the Union Bank, which was chartered in December 1832. On February 7, 1833, Thomas Patton Adams was voted in as a clerk of that new bank.[37] George Crockett Sr. was elected a director of the same institution. In November 1833, the Planters Bank was created. George Crockett was voted in as a director of that establishment on January 7, 1834.[38] With his uncle John a prominent banker in New York, it is not surprising that Thomas ended up in that profession also. Add in the connections to the Crocketts and Gibsons and one could see that Adams was positioning himself and his family for success.

Thomas Patton Adams performed well in his role at the Union Bank, and in 1837, he accepted the position of cashier of the Planters Bank in Pulaski, Tennessee, which meant he and his family would have to move.[39] He ventured south to scout out the new town and was the highest bidder for lot sixty-nine, which he bought for $305.[40] There would have been excitement in the Adams household in Nashville as the family prepared to leave. The young family packed their belongings, said goodbye to their friends and made their way south to another new beginning. The move allowed Thomas Patton to get himself and his family away from the filth of a growing, busy river city. His father had died fairly young, and this move would mean a fresh start and fresh air. Even at this point in his life, it is possible that Thomas Patton Adams was not healthy. Perhaps the rolling hills of Middle Tennessee, south of Nashville, reminded Thomas of the heather-clad hills of his Irish home. In any case, he and Anne and their children made their way south to Pulaski, more than seventy miles away.

Chapter 4

The Familiar Road

You can still trace the Adams family's movements south because today's Eighth Avenue was yesterday's Spruce Street that led to the Franklin Turnpike and then the Columbia Turnpike all the way to Pulaski, Tennessee. The turnpikes they used began as an act of the Tennessee legislature in 1829. The Nashville-Franklin Turnpike Company was formed, and work began soon thereafter.[41] Those turnpikes that linked Nashville to Franklin and continued to Pulaski are today known as U.S. Route 31. At a time when many people never left the county in which they were born, John Adams would travel far and wide: from Tennessee to New York to Mexico and New Mexico, then to Minnesota and Maryland, then to California and finally back to his homeland, the South. But of all those roads, trails and paths, the road that linked Nashville to Pulaski would become for John Adams the most familiar of his life.

When the Adamses departed Nashville, they passed by the old customs house as they left the city.[42] The family continued south and crossed the Harpeth River before entering the little town of Franklin. There were only a few buildings there then, but just south of Franklin to their right was a lovely new brick house owned by Fountain Branch Carter, and across the turnpike, to the Adamses' left, was a field where Mr. Carter would build a cotton gin. The beautiful countryside became hillier as they continued south. Leaving the little valley that enclosed Franklin, they passed through a narrow cut alongside Mr. Winstead's Hill. The road undulated over small rises as it curved to the right and passed over the West Harpeth River. Mr.

Thompson's house stood off to the right, in an area that, in the future, would become Thompson's Station when the railroad came through. The road straightened out and carried them on south through a little village called Spring Hill. The hills became more pronounced as they got closer to Columbia and then flattened out as they approached the Duck River. Once across the Duck, the road continued on to Pulaski. Their home was south of what is today the Courthouse Square, not too far from the Wertemberg Academy where young John Adams would soon be enrolled. The old school is no longer there; in its place is the Pulaski Recreation Center, which overlooks Maplewood Cemetery, where John Adams's travels would come to an end one day.

In the course of his lifetime, he would graduate from West Point with "Stonewall" Jackson and George McClellan, room with and be good friends with George Pickett and fight Indians alongside Colonel Thomas Fauntleroy and Kit Carson. His brother-in-law rode with Custer and was with the Seventh Cavalry at the Little Big Horn. And John Adams himself would ride into history on a dark November night in the fields south of Franklin, Tennessee, within yards of this same familiar road.

Chapter 5

"A Youth of Fine Talents"

In Pulaski, Thomas Patton went to work at the bank and Anne kept the house and reared the children. They acquired slaves who worked in and around the home and property. Mr. and Mrs. Adams enrolled John at Wertemberg Academy for the school year starting in 1838.[43] John Adams excelled at his studies. His math teacher, Benjamin Mitchell, wrote, "His capacity to learn is very good, and he acquires a knowledge of Mathematics with much more ease than most of the scholars whom I have instructed in that Branch of study. His natural disposition is good." His French instructor, Henry Masson, recalled Adams's "rapid improvement" in learning French. "He reads, translates and understands readily all that is placed in his hands written in that language."[44]

Thomas Patton Adams may have known his time was growing short, and as a result, he looked to the future and did what he could to set up his wife and children, including purchasing a life insurance policy. He also decided that John should go to the United States Military Academy at West Point and thus began the process of seeking an appointment for his son. John Adams's father had a penchant for making influential friends, and this would pay off now as he looked around for help. He called on United States representative Aaron Venable Brown, who carried the application process forward for John Adams. Congressman Brown represented Tennessee's Tenth Congressional District (which included Pulaski) and was a former law partner of a gentleman named James Knox Polk, who himself would soon rise to greatness. Brown wrote to the secretary of war, "He [Adams] is a young man of good morals and studious habits and I have no doubt, would acquit himself with credit and distinction—It would be a singular favour to him to procure such a situation, as his father has a large family and is in moderate circumstance. He is very desirous of such an advantage, as would be afforded him at West Point."[45]

Other friends of the family wrote letters of support for John Adams. We can learn of him through their eyes. Mr. J.B. Marshal described John Adams as "a youth of fine talents and of good family and character." Another wrote, "I take pleasure in saying that he is a youth of reputable family, and I have no doubt from his age and advancement in his studies that he is qualified, if appointed to discharge his duties well."[46] John Adams gained an appointment to the United States Military Academy at West Point. The then fifteen-year-old boy penned his acceptance, and his father endorsed the letter to Secretary of War John Bell:

> *Sir*
> *I had the honor to receive by the last mail through the Hon. A. V. Brown, a warrant appointing me to the vacancy in the Military Academy at West Point, from the 10th Congressional District of Tennessee. I accept the appointment with great pleasure and shall according to instructions, report myself at West Point between the 1st and 20th of June next—*
> *I have the Honor to be*
> *Being respectfully*
> *Your Obt St*
> *John Adams*
>
> *I hereby consent that my son John Adams shall enter into articles binding himself to serve eight years unless sooner discharged, at the military academy at West Point, according to the regulations of said academy.*
> *Tho. P. Adams*[47]

On April 10, 1841, a little more than one month after endorsing the letter that set in motion his son's destiny, Thomas Patton Adams died.[48] A newspaper account describes the cause of death as the result of an attack of "rheumatic or paralytic affection." The life insurance policy that he had taken out a few years before left his widow with $5,000.[49]

Springtime in Middle Tennessee is lovely. The green hillsides are flecked with the pinks and whites of dogwood blooms. New leaves of old trees fill up the empty spaces of winter. There are wildflowers of all colors and description popping up along the paths and fields and meadows. The warmth of April is so welcome, especially after a cold, harsh winter. But there would have been no joy in young John Adams's heart as he stood beside the grave of his father and contemplated the journey he was about to begin. A boy wants to please his father, even after—maybe especially after—the father's death. John Adams would not let his dad down. He would make this journey and see it through to the end, no matter where it led him. As he stood there, John Adams had no idea of the many miles he would roam before he, too, would come home to sleep beneath these same trees.

Chapter 6

Tough Going at West Point

From Pulaski, John Adams began his journey to West Point by traveling back up to Nashville along the same familiar road the family had first taken just a few years before. The trip could not have been an easy one. With his father's death fresh in his mind, not knowing what he was going to encounter in far-off New York, the fifteen-year-old boy bravely left the known for the unknown. He would never again live as a civilian in Tennessee.

The trip from Tennessee was a long and tiring one, involving river and road travel, and along the way he would have met people and seen cities and sights that were new to him. It was a preview of what was to come for John Adams—a life of travel and adventure, never staying in one place very long. Once in New York, Adams traveled up the Hudson River via steamboat to a landing below West Point. From there, he walked up a steep path to the highlands to the academy campus and grounds.[50] Unlike the gentle rolling hills and clear streams of his homeland, these hills were sharp and rocky and the river brown and slow moving. The famed author Charles Dickens visited West Point in the early 1840s. He claimed that the military academy "could not stand on more appropriate ground, and any ground more beautiful could not be."[51] Beautiful or not, it was a big change for the southern boy.

Adams was to be part of the class of 1845 and did his best to adjust to the new surroundings and demands of this world. As a new cadet, or "plebe," he would have heard the insults typically hurled at other plebes by upperclassmen: "animal," "thing," "reptile," "beast."[52] The plebes drilled twice a day and marched everywhere. Their newly issued blankets reeked

Cadet Memorial, West Point, where names of fallen cadets have been inscribed since 1817. *Library of Congress.*

of lanolin and so, along with all the other indignities the young men faced, they also stank. Food was boring and bland, and the new cadets had to eat quickly for fear an officer would bark out the command "squad rise" before they were finished.[53] Their meals consisted of bread and butter and hash (peeled potatoes cut and boiled in large iron kettles with chunks of meat left over from dinner the day before). Cooks added gravy for breakfast. For lunch, they might have beef with potatoes and sometimes boiled beef and rice. For supper, they dined on bread, butter and tea.[54]

The young men lit their rooms with whale oil lamps, which gave off a dim yellow glow and smelled bad. A plebe's room contained a two-foot square box into which all his belongings had to fit. In those barracks rooms, everything had to be in order. Bedsteads were to be against the farthest wall from the door. Tables had to be against that same wall, trunks stored under the bedsteads, lamps clean and on the mantel. Dress caps were to be arranged neatly on the shelf, and shoes, blacked, were to be carefully set out. The washstand was to be clean and in the corner. The looking glass stood between the washstand and the door. Books were arranged properly and placed on their shelf. Brooms were stored behind the door. Drawings and books were under the shelf. Cadets placed their muskets in the gun rack with locks sprung, bayonets in scabbards, accoutrements, sabers, cutlasses and swords hanging over the muskets. The box for scrubbing utensils was kept against the wall under the shelf nearest the fireplace. Clothes were hung neatly on pegs over the bedsteads, with the mattress and blankets neatly folded.[55] For any young person unused to this type of discipline, this could not be an easy transition.

In the winter, West Point had little access to the rest of the world because the Hudson River froze. There were no telegraph lines or railroads to the Point at that time. This could lead to a feeling of isolation and loneliness. John Adams, who turned sixteen on July 1, 1841, was not used to the discipline and requirements being placed on him. A typical day started at 4:00 a.m., when the morning gun fired to wake up the cadets. They were on the drill field by 5:00 a.m. Breakfast was at 6:30 a.m. Then back out to the parade ground at 8:00 a.m. Infantry or artillery drills lasted throughout the rest of the morning. Cadets marched back to the mess hall for lunch at 1:00 p.m. More military exercises followed in the afternoon. Parade at 6:00 p.m. and stag dances (no girls, of course) on the common until 9:00 p.m. Lights were to be out by 10:00 p.m.[56]

But John Adams liked to visit and talk with friends, rules or no rules. And this trait was not one that the Military Academy wished to encourage while school was in session. At West Point, cadets were "awarded" demerits for unacceptable behaviors. Demerits were given numeric values, and the total number of these demerit values was compiled and reviewed at the end of each year. For offenses of the first grade, a cadet received ten demerits. Offenses of the second grade earned eight. Third-grade offenses received five, and so forth to seventh grade, which earned the cadet one demerit. For example, an absence from reveille roll call was three demerits. Introducing spirituous liquors into barracks was eight demerits. Disobedience of the orders of a military superior was eight demerits.[57] The handbook stated, "When any cadet has a number expressing his demerit on the General Conduct Roll greater than two hundred for the year, such Cadet is declared deficient in conduct, and recommended by the Academic Board to the War Department for discharge."[58]

Adams's first full (called "fourth") year at the United States Military Academy saw him rack up 148 demerits. His conduct ranking was 201 out of 217 cadets at the academy, meaning of all the cadets in the United States Military Academy at that time, he ranked near the bottom in terms of his conduct. Some of the things young John Adams did to earn his dubious ranking that year included "allowing boisterous and profane swearing in quarters, 12 and 1 o'clock," "not complying with orders given him, to have hair cut" and "visiting after taps." He obviously had some trouble coping with the rigors and requirements of the school. Academically, however, Adams ranked thirty-sixth out of sixty young men in his class. He was thirty-third in math and eighteenth in French. (Mr. Masson of the Wertemberg Academy was right about John Adams's abilities with French and would have been proud.)[59]

During his next year, his third, Adams was discharged from the academy for "deficient" drawing. The academy emphasized drawing due to the fact that engineers needed to be able to draw maps and fortifications. Distraught, Adams sought help. There is no record of who intervened, but it is possible that one of his connected Tennessee friends came to his aid because John Adams did gain reappointment. Perhaps it was the commander of the cadets, a tall Tennessean named J. Addison "Ethical Tom" Thomas.[60] Or maybe it was thanks to help from a dear friend, Cave Couts. Adams was not the first nor would he be the last to be dismissed and reinstated. In any case, Adams had to redo his third class year. This negative had the effect, however, of placing Adams in what would become a very famous class: the class of 1846.

Chapter 7

"Far from Home"

One of Adams's best friends was an older classmate and fellow Tennessean, Cave Johnson Couts. Couts did not go on to gain fame as a soldier, although he went on to live a full and interesting life, ending up in California. He gained appointment to West Point through his uncle Cave Johnson, who would become postmaster general under President James Knox Polk. Couts graduated in 1843 and continued to encourage Adams.[61] Academically, Adams was fairly strong, but it was his conduct that hurt him. John Adams had friends. He was social and enjoyed the company of others. One of his friends, in fact his roommate at one time, was a young man whose name would become one of the most famous in all of American history: George Edward Pickett. Adams spoke of this friendship in a letter to Couts: "I am still living in 'B' camp on north side of South Barracks live with Pickett he is the best friend I have here and is very careful about getting demerit."[62] Apparently, young Pickett was not careful enough because, like Adams, the Virginian also liked to push the limits. Neither Pickett nor Adams did particularly well following rules, as their demerit records indicate.

The 1843 Conduct Roll listed Adams ranking as 193rd out of 223 total cadets with 124 demerits, while Pickett was 218th with 126. In 1844, Adams's ranking was 202nd out of 211 cadets with 191 demerits. Pickett's was 178th with 144 demerits. In 1845, Adams ranked 166th out of 204 with 132 demerits; Pickett was 189th with 158. And in their final Conduct Roll, 1846, Adams ranked 183rd out of 213 with 151 demerits and Pickett was 210th with 195.[63]

One of the activities Pickett enjoyed was sneaking away from the academy and going to a nearby tavern owned by Benny Havens. There is no record of Adams accompanying his friend, but one could imagine the young Tennessean and his roommate slipping out together from time to time. Benny Haven's tavern was so well known that the Marquis de Lafayette visited it in 1824, before his trip to Nashville, and ordered one of Benny's famous "hot flips." A few years after Lafayette's notable visit, a young cadet named Edgar Allan Poe often visited Benny's tavern. Poe said that Benny was "the only congenial soul in the entire God-forsaken place."[64] Never mind that getting caught at Benny's was an offense punishable by dismissal from the academy, Pickett snuck away and would often put his fine singing voice to use singing Benny's "anthem," which was set to the tune of "Wearin' of the Green":

> *Come, fill your glasses fellows, and*
> *Stand up in a row*
> *To singing sentimentally, we're going*
> *For to go;*
> *In the Army there's sobriety, promotion's*
> *Very slow,*
> *So we'll sing our reminiscences of*
> *Benny Havens, oh!*
> *Oh Benny Havens, oh! Oh, Benny Havens, oh!*
> *So we'll sing our reminiscences*
> *Of Benny Havens, oh!*[65]

Even if he did not slip away with his friend, Adams still managed to get into trouble. His more serious offenses included visiting at 11:30 p.m. and midnight (after lights out), "abusing a waiter in the mess hall by throwing a quantity of bread in his face," being found off limits at the public dock at 10:00 and 11:00 p.m., visiting at 10:00 p.m. and midnight, sitting down on post, being found off limits at the cascade at 9:30 and 11:00 p.m., leaving his post at 9:00 and 10:00 p.m. while on sentinel duty, neglect of duty as officer of the day, leaving guard room for more than twenty minutes at 2:00 and 3:00 p.m. and "questioning the authority of an officer who has made a just and proper report against him."[66] Adams got three extra Saturday guard duty turns and found himself confined to quarters for a week for the bread throwing incident in the mess hall.[67] The young man from Tennessee needed to improve his behavior. It was likely Couts who influenced his friend to finally buckle down. Adams wanted to do well for Couts.

Adams's self-described best friend and roommate at West Point, George Edward Pickett, who would gain everlasting fame at Gettysburg. *Library of Congress.*

In one letter Adams writes:

> *It is my intention to study hard enough to know my lesson if possible every day before going to the section room. So far this I have done am in hopes this will satisfy you my dear friend this much, at least, I promise you—I have had fewer demerits for these months past than ever since I have been here.... is it astonishing! Yet 'tis true have had to "bone" conduct though very hard to be so good a "boy" I have for the whole year.... Oh! But this is a dull and dreary place far from home and friends all those to me most near and dear.*[68]

In another letter he assured Couts that he had no intention "of being found" and went on to inform his friend that his marks, though not as good as Couts's, were improving.[69] (The classroom instructor would call a cadet to the blackboard at the front of the class. With a piece of chalk and a sponge, the cadet would be given a problem to solve in front of the class. If the young man did well and could keep his answer going until the bugle blew, this was known as "bugling" it. If he did not know the answer, that was a "fess." This was followed by a "found," which was a delinquency.[70] Adams determined to avoid that indignity.)

Adams also wrote of his daily life, "It's bitter cold and this old room on the north side of South Barracks is full of cracks and crevices which afford fine passage to the bleak north winds, all around is but one vast sheet of snow and ice."[71] In April 1845, he complained of having been very sick recently. "Never was so sick in my life got up at 'Surgeon's Call' to 'Wheaton it' but felt too ill to go,"[72] he wrote. (To "Wheaton it" was to get an excuse from the post physician, Dr. W.V. Wheaton.)[73] John Adams's grandfather died young. His own father died young. His illness here at West Point was the first of several severe sicknesses he would suffer throughout his life.

The year 1845 did not start well for the men and women who lived on that rocky plateau. The winter was cold, and illness claimed not one but two lives. The cannon-topped Cadet Memorial, erected in 1817 to honor fallen cadets, would soon have another name to add.[74] Samuel Raymond, nicknamed "Dad" because he was the oldest cadet in the class of 1846, got sick and died in January 1845. Hours before "Dad's" death, Luisa Weir, the wife of drawing instructor Robert Weir, passed away at age thirty-seven, having just given birth ten days before to a little girl.[75] The cadets made their way to the chapel to pay their respects. Even here, in this beautiful place, sorrow found its way.

During this time, John Adams fell victim to another kind of affliction: "dragoon fever." Many of the young cadets wanted to become dragoons. Trained to fight both on horseback and on foot, dragoons carried swords and short muskets, wore their hair a little longer and blazed frontier trails. In short, the dragoons seemed to offer an exciting life, different from the humdrum, *march, march, march* tedium of the structured world of West Point. Adams talked about this "fever" in other letters to his friend. "One of my greatest pleasures which I have to look forward to is that of getting in the 1st Dragoons….I should like very much to be out there with you so I will study hard and try to get in the Dragoons. Good bye and may heaven protect you in the fervent prayers of your far distant yet still true friend John."[76]

John Adams applied himself to the classwork, and his hard work paid off. He studied, attended classes and improved in the class ranking academically every year. Starting with his "do over" year, third class, 1844, he ranked thirty-third overall out of seventy-eight (twenty-second in math, twenty-third in French, fiftieth in drawing and thirty-third in English grammar). His second class year, 1845, Adams finished twenty-ninth out of sixty-two (fifteenth in philosophy, twenty-second in chemistry and fifty-fifth in drawing). And in his final or first class year, 1846, John Adams ranked twenty-fifth out of fifty-nine members (nineteenth in engineering, fourteenth in ethics, fifteenth in artillery, eighteenth in infantry tactics and twenty-fifth in mineralogy and geology).[77] In that final class year at West Point, John Adams had the privilege of studying under the famous tactician engineering professor Dennis Hart Mahan. Mahan's aim was to "rear soldiers worthy of the Republic." He believed in two important principles for military success: speed of movement and the use of reason. Adams would later display those traits, especially the use of reason.[78]

Of the fifty-nine young men who graduated in the class of 1846, ten would go on to become Confederate generals. Twelve would become Federal generals. Among the more famous names are Ambrose Powell "A.P." Hill, Thomas Jonathan "Stonewall" Jackson, George Brinton McClellan and George Edward Pickett.[79] At graduation, the cadets marched under the academy colors. Just a few short years earlier, these young men had appeared as boys on this plain and dressed up as soldiers. Now they were young officers, anxious to prove themselves "worthy of the Republic." In the distance, the academy band played as they marched, their music becoming more distinct as they approached, playing "Auld Lang Syne" and ending the ceremony with "Home Sweet Home."[80]

Chapter 8

The Road to War

After graduating from the United States Military Academy, the young men were brevetted second lieutenants and continued their service in the army. Their final class ranking determined their placement choices. The top graduates, such as George McClellan, became engineers. Graduates ranked fifth through eighth became topographical engineers ("topogs"). The next highest group was offered ordnance, then artillery, infantry and, lastly, mounted rifles of dragoon. Because of his class ranking, Adams qualified for artillery, but he petitioned for and received permission to serve in the dragoons.[81] He received his appointment as brevet second lieutenant, First Regiment Dragoons, on July 1, 1846, his twenty-first birthday.

He received the notification of his commission while at home in Pulaski, Tennessee, with his mother and other family members. The hero had returned, and there would have been suppers to attend, visits to make, friends to catch up with and stories to tell. These halcyon days could not last forever, and the happy reverie soon ended as he had to leave to continue his journey. Adams was to go to Fort Leavenworth, Kansas, to join up with Colonel Stephen Watts Kearney's Army of the West expedition to Santa Fe, New Mexico.[82] As he had done and would continue to do, John Adams prepared to leave.

Ultimately, Colonel Kearney and the Army of the West were headed to Mexico because the United States was at war with its southern neighbor. The war with Mexico was a final, terrible act in a long-simmering series of disputes, disagreements and lack of definition between the United States and Mexico that stretched back to the Louisiana Purchase. Although France and the United States made the deal in 1803, Spain and later Mexico believed that the disputed lands were their territory. The obvious fact that Native Americans had lived in these same lands for centuries added to the brewing conflict. In those years between the buy and the war, Americans sent a small expeditionary force under Zebulon Montgomery Pike to New Mexico to reconnoiter the lands. American businessmen then opened a successful trade route to Santa Fe. After gaining its independence from Spain, Mexico allowed a northern district, Texas, to be settled with American settlers who then fought for and gained independence from Mexico. Texas was later annexed by the United States; throughout all of these events, some of the prominent characters involved had direct or indirect ties to Adams and Tennessee. One of the fathers of Texas Independence was Adams's father's old acquaintance William Harris Wharton, who first helped the Texans gain their independence from Mexico and then later assisted with their annexation to the United States. Andrew Jackson played key roles in disputes with Spain and Mexico, and Sam Houston, another Tennessean, led the inspired Texan army to victory over Santa Ana at San Jacinto. James Knox Polk, friend of Representative Brown and Cave Couts's family, would lead the United States in its war with Mexico.[83]

By 1845, as Adams was continuing his schoolwork at West Point, the conflict between the United States and Mexico had reached the boiling point. After coming to power by overthrowing his predecessor, Mexican president Mariano Paredes vowed to maintain the border with his northern neighbor along the Sabine River. President James Knox Polk, after an unsuccessful attempt to buy the disputed lands, dispatched General Zachary Taylor to the Southwest with an army of four thousand men. As Taylor moved his army southward to the Rio Grande, Paredes dispatched troops northward to intercept the approaching Americans. Polk instructed Taylor not to treat the Mexicans as the enemy but to take "appropriate action" if shots were fired. The two armies met and drew up on opposite sides of the Arroyo Colorado, just north of the Rio Grande.[84] The two commanders exchanged terse communiques. The Americans finally splashed across the shallow stream, and the Mexicans withdrew to the south. Mexican general Pedro Ampudia, who was a veteran of the Alamo and San Jacinto, sent a message to Taylor that read, "Return to the east bank of the Nueces River while our governments are regulating the pending question to Texas." If Taylor refused, "arms and arms alone must decide the question."[85]

Although not related, Adams referred to James Knox Polk as "Uncle Jimmy" in letters to his friend Cave Couts. *Library of Congress.*

As the two sides tensely waited for the next move, the Mexican force was further strengthened with the arrival of General Mariano Arista. His men brought the total Mexican forces to eight thousand men against Taylor's four thousand. Arista did not waste time. He sent cavalry troops across the river. Taylor dispatched dragoons under Captain S.B. Thornton to contest the move. Thornton's contingent was surrounded, and several U.S. soldiers were killed in the fight. General Arista bragged, "I had the pleasure of being the first to start the war." Two weeks later, word reached Washington, D.C., of the fight. President Polk charged Mexico with shedding "American blood upon the American soil." Congress authorized the president to accept fifty thousand volunteers and $10 million for national defense. The war with Mexico had begun.[86]

Chapter 9

The Battle of Santa Cruz de Rosales

In the 1840s and 1850s, United States soldiers who were headed to the Southwest began their journey in the city of St. Louis. There they boarded a boat for transport. Depending on the time of year and the water level of the Missouri River, it might take a week to go from St. Louis to Fort Leavenworth in Kansas. However, sandbars, snags and low water levels could hang up a boat and delay the journey. At other times of year, high water or ice could pose travel hazards that interrupted the trip. And for many of the soldiers, including Adams, Fort Leavenworth was just the beginning. On his first trip to the Southwest, Adams traveled along the Santa Fe Trail and saw things that were all new to him, such as prairie dogs, pronghorns and rattlesnakes, which soldiers would sometimes find in their blankets after awaking from a night's sleep in the open. Another oddity for the men were mirages, which the soldiers called "false ponds." One soldier noted, after seeing his first mirage, "Nothing appears as it is. About a mile distant from us appeared a crystal lake, studded with numerous islands, so perfectly defined that no one could imagine it to be anything else than a real lake. Though prepared for the illusion, many of the men believed it real, bet upon it, and of course lost their bets." There were also distinct, distant landmarks such as Pike's Peak and, in the far distance, to the southwest, twin mountains called the Spanish Peaks, also known as "the breasts of the world."[87]

New Mexico had been settled by Europeans for more than two and a half centuries by the time Adams arrived for duty. In all that time, the Spanish and their descendants lived under near constant threat of raids by the Native

American tribes in the area. There were Utes, Cheyennes and Arapahoes to the north; Kiowas and Comanches to the east; and Apaches to the south. In time, the Comanches would become the most feared of all these tribes, known far and wide for their fierceness, but there were also Navajos, who were once the strongest and richest of all the tribes in the area. When the first Spaniards arrived in the late 1500s, they brought with them sheep and horses, two things many of the Native Americans would soon prize. The little Spanish *churro* sheep were suited for this harsh environment, and the introduction of the horse facilitated raiding. The Navajos in particular became expert raiders. (The Navajos already placed a high value on sheep. They used to put their children to bed at night, reminding them, "The sheep is your mother.") Because the Spanish-speaking people of the New Mexico territory were so far from Mexico City and the seat of power, they never really had the protection they wanted and needed.[88] Adams would later see this neediness firsthand when he was stationed in the territory after the Mexican War.

Named for Zebulon Montgomery Pike, Pike's Peak would by seen by thousands, including John Adams. *Library of Congress.*

John Adams became ill and could not report for duty with Kearney's Army of the West as planned. He was not well enough to resume active duty until January 1847. Once he did recover, Lieutenant Adams was detached to Santa Fe, New Mexico, under the command of Captain William Nicholson Grier. Adams was attached to Company I.[89] This command moved back and forth from Taos to Albuquerque. Once back in Albuquerque, Adams's duties included acting quartermaster and acting commissary of subsistence. (His brother Thomas Patton Adams would be commissary of subsistence on General Adams's staff during the Civil War.)[90] In these capacities, Adams saw to procuring and distributing supplies for the soldiers. During this time, he also escorted prisoners to Las Vegas, New Mexico, and took part in an expedition against an Indian chief named Cortes.[91]

The 1847 Army Regulations spell out the requirements and duties of quartermasters:

> *102…Appointments of regimental quartermaster will only be conferred upon officers who unite the experience, discretion, and qualification necessary for the efficient performance of their responsible and varied duties.*
>
> *103…Among these duties, are the laying out of the camps, care of the wages and camp equipage of the regiment; superintending the removal of obstructions in roads, during a march; being present at issues, and distributions, to judge of the quantity and quality of the supplies tendered; and the duties of Assistant Quartermaster at a post or station.*[92]

Adams continued to be an effective administrator and would soon be called upon to join an expeditionary force under the command of Colonel (later General) Sterling Price. Despite American success in the war, there were rumors of an imminent attack from Mexico. Price's force assembled in El Paso, Texas, and formed their invasion plans in February 1848. Price, a Virginian by birth, rose to prominence in Missouri. At the outbreak of the war with Mexico, Price was a United States representative from the Show Me State. A fellow Missourian, Senator Thomas Hart Benton, obtained a commission for Price to raise a regiment of men to fight in the war. Benton held a long-standing desire to expand the United States' influence and allow for freer trade to Mexico and beyond, and this war could help further his aims. In January 1847, Price's regiment put down an insurgency against American forces in Taos, New Mexico. Price's political friends used this victory to gain for him a brigadier general's commission. Others, notably professional soldiers, criticized his promotion, saying the action against the insurgency was a minor affair and there were other, more deserving officers awaiting promotion. It is possible that this criticism may have inspired Price to disobey War Department orders and proceed with his plan to find and attack a Mexican stronghold.[93] What he used as his official reason was a report (which turned out to be false) that reached Santa Fe in February 1848 that claimed a Mexican force of three thousand soldiers was marching north on Santa Fe.[94]

To meet this phantom threat, Price assembled a force that included Companies B, G and I First Dragoons under the command of Major Benjamin Lloyd Beall.[95] The artillery, in Company B, would be under the command of Lieutenant John Love, an experienced Indian fighter and a graduate of West Point, class of 1841.[96] Additionally, there were mounted volunteers from Missouri under Colonel John Ralls, Missouri Infantry (volunteers) under Lieutenant Colonel Alton R. Easton and volunteers from Santa Fe under Major Robert Walker.[97]

John Adams was named acting adjutant of the dragoons, serving directly under Major Beall. Price's army left Texas on March 1, 1848, bound for Chihuahua, Mexico.[98] The march into Mexico did not go well. Arriving first in El Paso, Texas, Price received orders from Adjutant General Roger Jones to stay in El Paso and send several hundred mounted troops to California, another territory the United States hoped to acquire. Price ignored these orders and went ahead with his own plans and plunged across the Rio Grande in pursuit of a Mexican invasion force that was not there.[99] Approaching Chihuahua, Price's small army received a contingent of mounted Mexican troopers who approached under a flag of truce to inform Price that they had a message from their governor, General Angel Trias. The dispatch advised Price that the Treaty of Guadalupe Hidalgo had been signed and the hostilities were at an end. The war was over. However, Price had not yet received official word from his own government, so he did not believe Trias. The Mexican governor, wanting to avoid an armed confrontation, abandoned Chihuahua and moved farther south to Santa Cruz de Rosales.[100]

Price moved to the outskirts of that town and positioned his men to attack. He demanded Trias surrender his forces unconditionally. Trias again reminded Price that the war was over. Price allowed for a period of five days to wait for a Mexican courier to obtain a copy of the armistice. This led nowhere, and Price, with no evidence to support Trias's claim, decided to attack the town.[101] Lieutenant Adams, with Beall's force, had been encamped more than two hundred miles away when they received orders to join Price at Santa Cruz de Rosales. They covered the distance in three and a half days.[102]

The town was on a plateau next to a clear running stream. Irrigation ditches surrounded the town, watering the adjacent fields. A Missouri Volunteer later wrote in his journal, "The cottonwoods were in full leaf; and the grass quite green; peas and other vegetables in full blossom."[103] In the middle of town was the plaza. A large Catholic church looked down over the inhabitants. Trias's men, eight hundred strong, were armed with old flintlock smoothbore rifles. He placed most of his men in the plaza to avoid direct gunfire. He posted his remaining troops on rooftops.[104]

On Thursday, March 16, 1848, more than a month after the war with Mexico officially ended, the Battle of Santa Cruz de Rosales began. Price's men made last-minute preparations for battle. Soldiers checked their weapons and waited for the order to move forward. The Mexicans in the town nervously waited for the firing to begin. At last, the battle opened with a duel between American and Mexican artillery. Gun tubes roared as the powder inside exploded, launching deadly projectiles toward their intended targets. Shot and shell smashed into the walls of the town, and the Mexicans' replies tore into the fields, shredding the earth. Smoke clouded the scene. After several hours of artillery fire, the town remained in Mexican hands. Price then determined to assault Santa Cruz de Rosales with an infantry advance.[105] Around three thirty in the afternoon, the American artillery began firing again and American troops moved forward. Beall ordered Adams to report to Lieutenant Love to assist with orders and organization. According to Lieutenant Love's after-action report, during "the hottest of the fight" Adams volunteered to command a twenty-four-pound howitzer section. Adams's job, as the American infantry advanced, was to keep the housetops cleared of enemy soldiers.[106]

The strongholds in the town were the church and a two-story house. Mexican soldiers in the house did not put up much of a fight, but the soldiers in the church continued to fire away at the U.S. troops. There was a brief scare during the day when American scouts reported nine hundred lancers were fast approaching, threatening Price's position. Mexican cavalrymen, armed with lances, had shown themselves to be deadly foes. The supposed relief force turned out to be local inhabitants of the surrounding areas, who heard the gunfire and were curious to see what was going on.[107] The fighting continued. Adams's howitzer sent two shells into the enemy combatants on the church roof. The second shell exploded among the defenders, and the survivors fled their position and scattered for cover. Another shell from Adams's howitzer struck an ammunition wagon, causing a terrific explosion. The American troops moved forward. Muskets crackled up and down the

A highly stylized rendition of a dragoon charge during the war with Mexico. *Library of Congress.*

lines as the artillery pounded away at the Mexican defenders. When the sun set, the acrid air cooled a bit, but the firing continued. Finally, around 9:00 p.m., the Mexicans surrendered. The Americans possessed the town.[108]

Here was young John Adams's first experience with real war. This was not the studied, written-about war in textbooks. This was filth and blood, screaming and explosions, noise and smoke, stench and death, and he did not flinch or disappoint. He stood firm. He directed accurate fire. He helped win this battle. Captain Beall later reported why he had dispatched Adams to Love: "I felt confident that his services would be more important with that command, as the acting sergeant major could convey all the necessary orders to the different commanders of companies under my command. In this supposition I was not disappointed, as Lieutenant Adams was placed in command of a 24-pound howitzer, which did great execution upon the enemy's batteries and town, causing an explosion of one of his ammunition wagons, or caissons."[109] For his actions that day, John Adams was brevetted first lieutenant for his "gallant and meritorious service."[110]

The Americans lost no more than five men killed. The Mexicans sustained much more severe losses, as more than two hundred of their soldiers were killed.[111] All of those men died in a war that was already over.

Chapter 10

Frontier Duty

"The Orphans of Chihuahua"

After the battle, Adams and Company I, First Dragoons, continued to serve in and around Chihuahua, Mexico, and Adams caught up with his old friend Cave Couts. The two Tennesseans, long separated, were together once more. They had much to talk about. Adams had not let his friend down, had graduated and now was a battle-hardened veteran with stories of his own to tell. What a joyous reunion that must have been. In a letter to Adams's former artillery commander, John Love, Couts referred to this time: "I have come this far with the Capts. Whiltsey [Joseph Hotchkiss Whittlesey] and Adams—the orphans of Chihuahua." (Neither Whittlesey nor Adams was actually captain at the time.)[112] In the same letter, Couts inquired about the alleged massacre that took place after the Battle of Santa Cruz de Rosales. He was relieved to learn that the regulars played no part in it. "We are delighted to hear from Capt. Grier that you had nothing to do with the 'Cow Pen Slaughter' at Santa Cruz. Something had been heard of it previous to the arrival of the Capt. which agreed with his version of the affair, viz, you penned up a number of Mexican regular greasers, and slaughtered them by file. We are all proud, and feel happy in learning that you gave countenance to no such inhumanity."[113] Couts concluded the letter with a hint that John Adams and his fellow young officers whiled away some of the long hours in Mexico with distilled spirits: "I had forgotten at the commencement of my letter to congratulate you on your Captaincy—allow me to do so, in a few minutes, with a good gulp of Puros (1200) Ano, not at least a keg of fine old Brandy (15 galls). Take a drink with all the fellows in Chihuahua also, for me."[114]

Adams resumed his duties as acting adjutant to the dragoon command in Chihuahua until July 1848, when he and his men were ordered back to the United States. His friend First Lieutenant Joseph Whittlesey was his commander. The 320-mile march back to the United States took fifteen days. Upon returning, Adams resumed quartermaster and commissary duties.[115] Major Beall recognized Adams's administrative talents and liked the handsome young Tennessean. He brought Adams in to be his adjutant again, and they reunited in Taos, New Mexico. As Beall's assistant, Adams handled correspondence and letters for his commander and later participated in an expedition against Kiowa Indians.[116]

Throughout the West and Southwest, American settlers continued to move onto lands inhabited by Native Americans. Inevitably, there was contact with Native American tribes. Sometimes these encounters ended in bloodshed. Whenever reports of hostile Indian activity reached dragoon outposts, the officer in charge would be compelled to investigate. One such report led Major Beall to form a small force to check out reports of aggressive actions of some Kiowa Indians. Adams's Company, I, under the command of First Lieutenant Whittlesey, headed north for Bent's Fort and the Kiowas.

This was a new experience for Adams—his first visit to an Indian encampment. Riding into the Kiowa camp, the dragoons were on the alert for trouble but found it to be peaceful. Beall called for a council of the principal chiefs of five different tribes who were present in the area at the time. Each contingent brought with it its own unique dress and culture. Adams watched and learned as Beall made his way among the men of the various tribes. In the council were seven Kiowas, six Arapahoes, two Cheyennes, two Apaches and four Comanches. Beall calmly explained to the chiefs that the war between the United States and Mexico was over, and the road from Santa Fe was not to be molested. The chiefs pledged peace and friendship. There was no needless bloodshed, no loss of innocent lives. Adams witnessed the power of reason.[117]

While Adams continued his work as an adjutant to Beall, he also took part in other expeditions against Indian tribes, including the Apaches, Comanches, Navajos, Utes and Kiowas. Some of these encounters escalated into shooting skirmishes. Reason first, but if necessary, do not hesitate to use force.[118] Aside from the occasional fight, life as a dragoon was fairly boring. Each dragoon company, when at full strength, had a captain, a first lieutenant, a second lieutenant, four sergeants, four corporals and forty-eight privates.[119] The men carried weapons that included carbines, horse pistols and, later, short muskets called musketoons. Dragoons also carried sabers, which they referred to as "old wristbreakers" because they were heavy and difficult to use. When fully equipped, the dragoon might carry as much as eighty pounds of weapons, clothing, blankets and other items. A message sent to the president of the United States in 1851 lists dragoon equipment and armament:

> *Musketoon = 6 lb 8 oz*
> *Aston pistol = 2 lb 8 oz*
> *Sabre, sabre belt, cartridge box, sling and swivel, and sabre knot = 8 lb 4 oz*
> *Forty rounds ammo = 3 lb 0 oz*
> *Holster complete = 2 lb 8 oz*
> *Curry comb and brush = 1 lb 8 oz*
> *Spurs and straps = 8 oz*
> *Two blankets (Horse and bed) = 9 lb 0 oz*
> *Valise containing one pair wool overalls, one pair of drawers, one flannel shirt, one pair of stockings, one fatigue frock = 6 lb 4 oz*
> *Great coat = 6 lb 4 oz*
> *Nose bag = 1 lb 4 oz*
> *Picket pin and rope = 3 lb 0 oz*
> *Total = 78 lb 0 oz*[120]

Reveille sounded at dawn. The men stirred awake and assembled for roll call. After roll call came stable call when the dragoons tended to their horses, feeding and watering them. Dragoons had to be attentive to their mounts because if the horse failed in battle or on the march, the dragoon suffered the consequences. After seeing to their horses, there was sick call. Sick soldiers reported to the post surgeon for exam and treatment. Breakfast was usually served around 7:30 a.m. After breakfast came "fatigue call," which is when daily work assignments were made. These "fatigue" tasks included construction, cutting and hauling wood, working at the sawmill, cleaning the post grounds, loading and unloading supplies, building roads and tending the post's gardens. Guard duty was scheduled on a rotating basis. Guards were not expected to do any other fatigue duties. Guards worked twenty-four-hour shifts with three reliefs during the twenty-four hours. Drills were done once or twice per week. When drills were conducted, they occurred at 10:00 a.m. and sometimes after lunch. After the drills, the dragoons went back to their assigned work tasks. Lunch was at noon, and evening mess time was determined daily, based on when that day's work had been completed. Before lowering the flag at sunset, there would be a final roll call for the day. After that, the dragoons were expected to be in their quarters unless they were on leave or guard duty. Enlisted men slept in the crowded and uncomfortable squad room. The men slept two to a bed, head to toe, and used rolled-up coats as pillows. The good news was the dragoons were required to bathe once a week and wash their feet twice a week. The officers fared better, but the heat and the dust and the danger of the patrols were all shared.[121]

Chapter 11

A Memorable Mess Mate

In January 1849, John Adams was promoted to adjutant of dragoons in New Mexico and continued to work for his mentor, Major Benjamin Lloyd Beall.[122] According to the *Biographical Register of the Officers and Graduates of the United States Military Academy*, Adams took part in a skirmish with Native Americans at El Cerro de la Olla, New Mexico, on March 13, 1849, and skirmished with Apaches at Tuccuncurre Butte in November of the same year.[123] In June 1850, Adams reported to Santa Fe, seventy miles south of Taos, where he took temporary command of Company K, Second Dragoons. From there, Adams moved back to Taos, then Ceboleta, Albuquerque and once again Santa Fe.[124] Also in June, Adams received orders to move to the post at Rayado, New Mexico, because of a recent Indian raid. Natives had attacked and stolen many head of livestock.

Founded by mountain man Lucien Maxwell in 1848, the little village along the Rayado River would be subject to Indian attacks from nearby Apaches and Utes but would survive thanks, in part, to Maxwell's decision to bring in his friend Christopher Houston "Kit" Carson to help with security issues. Carson, though just five feet four inches, was legendary among the whites and the Native Americans as a tracker, hunter and fighter.[125] Carson's mere presence lent credibility to the enterprise and provided protection in case there was actual fighting. Maxwell's ranch would become a famous stop on the Santa Fe Trail as trade goods continued to move into the area. There was a definite strategic importance to this area, and Adams was part of the effort to keep it safe.[126] One of the dragoons described the area around the

Christopher Houston "Kit" Carson rode with Adams in pursuit of hostile Native American warriors. *Library of Congress.*

Rayado this way: "The place is situated on the edge of the great plains at the foot of the 'eternal snow clad hills' a spur of the Rocky Mountains. A beautiful stream arises a few miles above the town in the mountains and winds its serpentine course downward until it is lost in the great, dry, wide plain below the village."[127]

Within thirty minutes of arriving at Rayado, Adams received orders to return to Las Vegas, where a larger force was being raised by Major William

Nicholson Grier, comprising three dragoon companies, G, I and K, along with one hundred Mexican volunteers. Once assembled, Grier's force pursued the hostiles who had attacked the post at Rayado. It took them three days, but the Americans caught up to the Indian forces, inflicted several casualties and recovered much of the stolen livestock.[128]

After the successful expedition, Adams received orders to return to Las Vegas and assume permanent command of Company K, First Dragoons. Adams was a dedicated soldier, but he was now sick and in need of an overdue leave. Grier and Adams protested the move to Las Vegas. Grier did not want to lose his valuable, trusted adjutant, and Adams needed a leave of absence.[129] Adams's and Grier's protests went unanswered, and the ill Tennessean assumed command. Although sick, Adams did his duty. He looked after his men, and as a new commander, he grew concerned about the fact that his dragoons were being used for fatigue duty while the infantrymen at the post were allowed to do nothing. From November 1850 to January 1851, Lieutenant Adams filed official protests regarding this situation. He received no reply.[130]

In March, he filed a request to allow his men to move from Las Vegas due to a lack of fresh meat and vegetables. Headquarters agreed to the extent that they would allow Adams to send out sorties to search for supplies.[131] In response, Adams led a group in search of food. While crossing the Arkansas River, one of the supply wagons became entangled, and when Adams attempted to save the wagon, he injured his arm severely enough that it took four months to heal. He applied for leave to recover. The request was denied. Headquarters could not spare him, or any officers, for that matter.[132]

Adams stayed at his post, and by June, he was well enough to ride again. He received notification that a local sheriff had requested assistance in arresting some Mexican citizens. Adams investigated and found that three people were being held for arrest by the sheriff for attempting to incite the local Mexican people to rise up against the Americans. Having heard the evidence, Adams concluded that the alleged troublemakers were the victims of political intrigue. He took them with his men back to Las Vegas. On the way back, Adams went from village to village, in his words, "in order to show them how readily in like cases the troops would move." He also "attempted to prove to them the impropriety and utter futility of attempting an insurrection."[133]

It was not unusual for Adams to receive reports of alleged thievery that proved to be untrue. In one case, local villagers ran toward Adams, crying, "The Indians have run off all our cattle!"[134] The lieutenant calmly questioned the agitated townsfolk. They all agreed that fourteen Indians had made off with their cattle. He then asked the hundred or so men assembled there, "Why don't you go bring them back? There are only fourteen Indians." The men declined to answer. Adams selected ten of his men to chase down the alleged thieves but told the villagers that if he found out that the charges were false, he would have the person who first brought in the report whipped. The villagers looked around and said that maybe the Indians hadn't really done anything wrong after all.[135]

As the dragoons traveled the New Mexico Territory, they would make camp after a long day of pursuing hostiles or looking for supplies and break into small groups, called "messes." Gathered around campfires, preparing food and coffee, they would talk about what they had seen and done that day and, of course, home. On one of these expeditions, Lieutenant Adams struck up a conversation with a mess mate named Charles McDougall. McDougall was a career soldier and surgeon. (One of the patients Dr. McDougall treated over the course of his work was Mrs. Anne Marshall, a sister of Robert E. Lee. The Virginian who would go on to become one of the greatest commanders in American history never forgot the doctor's care and attention to his ill sister. U.S. Grant was also a good friend of the surgeon.)[136] McDougall and Adams may have first met at West Point when the Tennessean was a cadet and McDougall was a post physician. Now, far away from the hills of New York, they met for sure, shared stories and developed a friendship that would last a lifetime. McDougall liked the handsome young southerner, and their talks would have included details about their families.[137]

Dr. Charles McDougall, Adams's father-in-law and dear friend. After the war, he invited Georgiana and her children to come home. *Library of Congress.*

Charles McDougall had met and married Maria Griffith Hanson in Indianapolis, Indiana. Because he was a military man, the family moved about the country as his duties required. Charles and Maria McDougall had four children: Georgiana, Josephine, Francis Pamela and Thomas Mower. At their various posts, officers referred to the McDougall children as "the four boys": "Georgie," "Joe," "Frank" and Thomas.[138] Georgiana was born at

Fort Winnebago in what was then the Michigan Territory, now Wisconsin, on May 1, 1835.[139] (A note about her baby brother: Thomas Mower "Tom" McDougall would, like his father, join the army. Tom was with George Armstrong Custer and the Seventh Cavalry at the Little Big Horn. Fortunately for Tom, he was in charge of the pack train and, therefore, survived the battle.)[140]

Georgie would have been fifteen or sixteen years old when she first met John Adams, and this beautiful young lady caught the attention of the dashing young officer, ten years her senior. The one known photograph of Georgiana shows her with her hair pulled back, revealing a lovely face with fine features. We can only imagine their walks in the twilight or the suppers John shared with the McDougalls. At some point, it became evident that John Adams and Georgiana McDougall would become more than friends.

In January 1852, word came from Washington, D.C., that Adams had been promoted to first lieutenant and ordered to report to duty with Company D, First Dragoons, at Fort Snelling in the Minnesota Territory. He departed for Minnesota in February 1852 and arrived there in May 1852.[141] Coincidentally, Charles McDougall was also transferred to Fort Snelling.[142]

Chapter 12

Minnesota and Marriage

Fort Snelling, Minnesota, was the northernmost outpost along the "Permanent Indian Frontier" that stretched all the way to Fort Jessup in Louisiana. Colonel Josiah Snelling completed the fort on the one-hundred-foot-high bluff that overlooks the confluence of the Minnesota and Mississippi Rivers in 1823 and named it St. Anthony. Built of log and stone and looking more like a medieval castle with towers on each of the four corners, the fort was renamed Snelling in 1825. Its original purpose was to guard against Indian troubles and keep the Dakota Sioux and Chippewas (also known as Ojibwas) from fighting each other. As the nation expanded westward, the action moved to the Great Plains, and Fort Snelling became a supply depot. When John Adams arrived, it was nearing the end of its useful life as a frontier outpost.[143]

Lieutenant Colonel Francis Lee commanded Fort Snelling at the time of Adams's arrival. John Adams was placed in command of the troopers in Company D, First Dragoons, and also served as the post adjutant. Up to this point in his career, he tended to be given administrative roles, and this continued in Minnesota. He must have been good at those duties or he would not have been assigned the important, although likely tedious, job.[144] When not dealing with post matters, Adams dealt with grievances that arose between the Dakotas and the Ojibwas. Fortunately, there were no serious Indian troubles during Adams's time in Minnesota.

Lieutenant Adams had not had an extended leave for six years. In September 1852, he was granted that long overdue leave and headed

Left: The only known photograph of John and Georgiana Adams, taken in 1858. John and Georgiana loved each other to the end. *Photo in author's possession.*

Below: Fort Snelling, Minnesota, where John and Georgiana Adams married in 1854. *Library of Congress.*

home to Tennessee, where he spent most of his time in Nashville, although he did travel to Pulaski to visit his mother and to Memphis to see his sister Martha and her husband, Thomas Eldridge. He did not return to the fort until early June of the following year.[145] When Adams got back to Fort Snelling, Minnesota had a new governor, Willis Arnold Gorman, who was also superintendent of Indian Affairs. Gorman met with Adams in July 1853. The new governor obviously liked the Tennessean because by October Adams had a new position and title: colonel of Minnesota Militia and aide-de-camp to Governor Gorman.[146] During Adams's time at Fort Snelling, he commanded only one expedition. In April 1854, Adams received word that a group of Dakota Sioux Indians had murdered a white settler. Adams and Company D left the fort to pursue the Indians. After a seventy-mile march, they caught up with and captured the Sioux. They returned the prisoners to the fort and waited for further instructions. Within a week, orders came to return the Indians to their own country.[147] Also in April, Adams received orders to depart on May 1 and take Company D back to the New Mexico Territory. The dragoons did not leave until May 6. Perhaps it was because their commander, Lieutenant Adams, had one other very important matter to attend to before he left. On May 4, 1854, John Adams married Georgiana McDougall.[148]

Chapter 13

Volatile New Mexico

The young couple, accompanied by Company D, First Dragoons, departed Minnesota aboard the *Minnesota Belle*. The Adamses and the company of dragoons arrived at Fort Leavenworth, the first stop on their journey, on May 17, 1854.[149] Adams took a short leave with his bride and returned in June to Fort Leavenworth, where he joined up with Colonel Thomas Turner Fauntleroy, who was assembling dragoons for a march to Fort Union in the New Mexico Territory.[150] Georgiana accompanied her new husband and the troops as they marched south to Council Grove, where they picked up the main Santa Fe Trail, which led them all the way to New Mexico. Crossing streams and miles of seemingly endless prairie, the troops pressed on toward their goal. Along the way, they ran into a party of mounted Kiowas who seemed intent on stealing their horses but did nothing. Adams's men, fresh from garrison duty, were unaccustomed to the tough going of life in the field, traveling, tending to their horses and being on constant lookout for trouble, and the march toughened them.[151]

Fort Union had been established by Lieutenant Colonel Edwin Vose Sumner, First Dragoons, in 1851 to protect the Santa Fe Trail from Apaches and Utes. Sumner had been in the army since 1819 and had a loud, booming voice. He was known as "Bull Sumner" and the "Bull of the Woods." He would later serve in the United States Army during the Civil War.[152] Sumner set up Fort Union to be a replacement location for departmental headquarters, which were then in Las Vegas, twenty miles away. Although "Las Vegas" is translated by some as "the meadows," "Bull" Sumner referred to it as a "sink of vice and extravagance."[153]

This picture was taken twenty years after Adams's service in New Mexico and gives a feel for the harsh environment faced by soldiers. *Library of Congress.*

New Mexico was more volatile than when Adams left. At first, the Native Americans had mostly tolerated the trickle of settlers and traders coming down the Santa Fe Trail. Now, as the trickle became a flood, the Indians were becoming more hostile and active.[154] In the first six months of 1854, right up to the arrival of Adams and his dragoons, there had been severe fighting with the Jicarilla Apaches at the Congillon River, Cieneguilla, Ojo Caliente and Sapello Creek. Wagon trains had been attacked, settlers slaughtered and women captured and sometimes raped. These outrages prompted reprisal attacks by the U.S. troops, and by June 1854, the territory was reeling from fighting and bloodshed.[155]

From Fort Union, Adams was ordered on to recently established Fort Craig on the tableland next to the Rio Grande, near the northern end of the *Jornada de Muerto* ("Journey of the Dead Man").[156] There were troubles with many Native Americans who were desperate for food, and two tribes, the Utes and Apaches, joined together and began stealing livestock to survive. Outrage also contributed to the decision by the Utes, under Chief Tierra Blanca, or "Blanco," to fight the whites.

Kit Carson warned the superintendent of Indian Affairs, David Meriwether, that the Utes were desperate for food and also unhappy they had not been receiving presents from the U.S. government at a time when tribes to the north were being given gifts. Carson wrote to Meriwether, advising the superintendent to meet with the Utes and distribute coats and shirts before winter. Carson's note ended with the statement, "I deem this to be a matter of great importance."[157] Meriwether agreed and, at the council with tribal representatives, distributed blanket coats to several in attendance. Unfortunately, everyone who received a coat died from smallpox not long thereafter, and the Utes believed that they had been intentionally poisoned. Chief Blanco of the Mohuache Utes then led a group to a community called Hardscrabble (later Pueblo), Colorado, on Christmas Day 1854. After entering the fort peacefully and participating in friendly games, Blanco and the Native Americans then grabbed their guns and began blazing away, leaving fifteen men dead, two women captured and all the livestock run off.[158] When news of this terrible attack reached the army, Adams and his men were ordered to report to Colonel Fauntleroy in Taos.[159] The colonel went to work and brought together a force of five hundred men, which included five companies of New Mexico volunteers. Fauntleroy departed on March 14, 1855. Kit Carson guided the force into the San Luis Valley. They were searching for a band of Utes and Jicarillas under the command of Chief Blanco. The American force moved north through snow and freezing weather in pursuit of the hostiles.[160]

They found the Indians camped along the Saguache Creek. The Native American warriors spotted the approaching danger and formed a line of battle to defend their camp. Chief Blanco, in a distinctive red shirt, urged on his men. The volunteers did not wait for orders and attacked. There was a wild firefight as the Indians fiercely defended their position. Over the din of battle, the army bugles sounded, announcing the arrival of the regulars, including Adams and his dragoons. Upon hearing this, the Indians headed for the mountains, leaving behind eight dead warriors. Fauntleroy lost two men killed.[161] Before pursuing the fleeing Indians, Fauntleroy moved his large force to Fort Massachusetts, in today's southern Colorado, to re-equip. After replenishing their supplies and preparing for the next movement, Fauntleroy split his forces in two, each pursuing Chief Blanco and his followers. Kit Carson took three companies of the volunteers and headed east of the Sangre de Cristo ("blood of Christ") Mountains. They found a camp and attacked, killing six Indians, wounding seven and capturing more than thirty horses. Carson's contingent suffered no casualties.[162]

Meanwhile, Fauntleroy's group had headed north and also found an encampment of hostiles. The Americans snuck up on the unsuspecting warriors and charged in. When the fighting ended, fifty Utes lay dead. Fauntleroy lost one man killed and two wounded. This startling and humiliating defeat broke the will of the Utes.[163] Adams likely missed this fight because, while in the field with Fauntleroy, he asked for and received permission to leave because Georgie was about to give birth to their first child. Despite his efforts to be there for the birth, Charles McDougall Adams, born on April 5, 1855, was waiting for him when he arrived.[164] The young father was not quite thirty years old. His beautiful young bride was almost twenty. There would have been congratulations around the camp. The Tennessean had a son.

For his generosity, however, Fauntleroy was reprimanded for allowing Adams to leave while the dragoons were in the field.[165] Adams rejoined the dragoons in Taos in May. From there, they first moved to Fort Union and then to Rayado, searching for Apaches. After scouting the area, they determined there was no danger. Adams marched back to Fort Union and wound up the expedition by returning to Fort Craig, where Georgie and little Charles waited.[166] Adams lost only one man killed during all the expeditions and marches into hostile territory. He and his men had covered nearly two thousand miles. Always an effective administrator, Adams also demonstrated once again that he could perform well in the field. For his remarkable work during these expeditions, Adams was brevetted captain in March 1856. He also received a letter of commendation from the Department of New Mexico. He was officially commissioned to captain on November 30, 1856.[167] The years he had spent in the Southwest had been good ones for John Adams. He met his wife there. They had their first child there. He had been reunited with Couts and made new friends, and now he was gaining a promotion.

While at Fort Craig, Adams received orders to report to Carlisle Barracks, Pennsylvania, for recruiting service. He left New Mexico in May 1856 and headed east. He reported in at Carlisle Barracks in July.[168]

Chapter 14

Recruiting Duty, Loss and Joy

John Adams and his family traveled from the New Mexico Territory to Carlisle Barracks, near Carlisle, Pennsylvania. There he received instructions to proceed on to Baltimore, Maryland, another ninety miles away, and set up a rendezvous station for recruiting.[169] In his role as recruiting officer, Adams's tasks included interviewing potential dragoon candidates, swearing in new recruits and making sure a surgeon determined if the men were physically fit. Once the potential dragoon passed the prerequisites, he swore an oath of allegiance to the United States of America. Then, the training process began, which Adams also oversaw.[170] By the 1850s, "dragoon fever" had cooled. In fact, when a contemporary of John Adams, Percival Green Lowe, joined the dragoons in 1849, the recruiting officer told him, "If you take this step, you will regret it only once, and that will be from the time you become acquainted with your position until the day you get out of it."[171]

Riding all day chasing Indians, performing the hard manual labor of fatigue duty at some distant outpost far from nearby towns and entertainment (and women) no longer seemed as exciting to young men. Therefore, by the time John Adams went to Baltimore to recruit, the fellows who showed up at the rendezvous were not the elite of society. Lowe recounted that "the fact that a man would get drunk was no bar to his enlistment, and his moral character was of little interest."[172] Once selected, recruits would drill, on foot, in the morning with saber and carbine and then drill on horseback in the afternoon.[173]

Adams accepted his commission as captain and, from Baltimore, traveled to our nation's capital, Washington, D.C., where he contracted an illness called "National Hotel Disease." It was rather serious and caused the patient to suffer a fever and "loss of flesh."[174] He was well enough, apparently, to tend to his husbandly duties because on November 19, 1856, Thomas Patton Adams, John and Georgie's second child, was born in Baltimore, Maryland.[175] As he had done out west, Adams continued to do his work even as he battled illness. He was the recruiting officer from July 1856 until August 1858. In that time, his station recruited more than two hundred men into the ranks.[176] In 1858, Captain Adams received orders to begin preparing for an expedition to California with his former commander, Colonel Fauntleroy. The plan called for Adams to travel to Memphis, proceed to Fort Smith, Arkansas, and then go to New Mexico and on to California. Adams, as ordered, made the preparations, but the expedition was called off. Adams, however, was still to proceed to California.[177]

While in Baltimore, word reached John Adams of his mother's death back home in Pulaski, Tennessee. Anne Tennant Adams passed away on February 14, 1858. Since leaving home in the summer of 1841, John Adams had rarely seen his mother. Now she was gone forever.[178] With both parents now deceased, John Adams, from Baltimore, did what he could to take care of his unmarried sister, Anne. He completed paperwork in June whereby he and brothers Crockett and Thomas Patton transferred their inherited property to sister Anne. The paperwork read:

> *Know all men by these presents that one John Adams, Thomas P Adams and Crockett Adams for and in consideration of the love and affection we have and bear towards our sister Ann* [sic] *T Adams, do hereby give grant alien, and convey to her and her heirs and assigns forever, our individual interest being one seventh each, in certain real estate in the town of Pulaski, which descended to us as children and heirs of Thos P Adams and Ann Adams dec'd, consisting of the block of lots on which is situated the Homestead, lately occupied by our mother the said Ann Adams, and three large lots lying south west of the Homestead, and known on the plan of the town as large lots No 66, 67, and 68. To have and to hold the same to the said Ann T Adams her heirs and assignees forever.*[179]

Brother Nathan, who was a lawyer, was not included in this loving transfer. John Adams recalled that his brother was "always scarce of money and hard pushed." His sisters did not approach Nathan for money because of what they described as "dread." "He bore such things badly and was apt to become excited and to put off such things," they later recalled. John Adams took leave in October 1858 and visited his sister Martha in Memphis and then went on to Pulaski to meet with his brother Nathan. John Adams was concerned for Anne's welfare and spoke to Nathan about his desire to "make provisions for Miss Anne's support, and about the sale of a part of the homestead at Pulaski to Nathan." John Adams intended to "close up the matter" with his older brother, but according to court documents, Nathan would turn out to be a disappointment in carrying out these wishes, as he never paid any of his brothers the money owed them.[180] This rift carried over to the Civil War. As late as April 1864, when John Adams and his men were fighting for what was left of the crumbling Confederacy, Anne's welfare was still a priority to him. Adams told his brother-in-law Thomas Eldridge that when the war was over he "would not hesitate to take steps to enforce the payment by Nathan of what he owed her [Anne] for the part of the estate bought by him [Nathan]."[181]

At the time of her death, John Adams's mother owned six slaves. They were Tom (who died soon after the death of Mrs. Adams), Quilla, Ursula, Mary, Tempy and Agnes. The slaves were not freed by the death of Anne. Ursula was sent to Memphis to John's sister Martha. Mary, Tempy and Agnes were hired out at eight dollars per month, the money going to John's sister Anne. The fate of Quilla, who was described as old, a drunkard and "not worth much," is not known. (One of Ursula's children, Maurice Adams Cleveland, would learn to read and write thanks to Nathan Adams's wife, Susan Louisa Pankey Adams. Mr. Cleveland became an educator for African American children in Pulaski after the Civil War.)[182]

The time in the East saw some dark days for John Adams, including the death of his mother and the terrible illness he suffered. But there were joys as well. John and Georgie Adams welcomed two new additions to their family during their time on the East Coast. In addition to the birth of Thomas Patton Adams, John Adams was born in Washington, D.C., on May 15, 1858.[183] In November 1858, Adams and his growing family left for California, where he would assume command at Fort Crook.

Chapter 15

The Decision

Captain John Adams, his wife and children and a detachment of recruits for the Sixth Infantry departed from Fort Columbus, New York, on November 2 and arrived at the Presidio in San Francisco on December 15, 1858.[184] By the late 1850s, it was possible to travel from New York to San Francisco in around thirty days due to steamship travel, which transported passengers from New York or California to Panama. From there, the travelers made their way across the isthmus on foot, by coach or via a train that carried them to another steamship that would take them to their destination.[185]

The discovery of gold in California in 1849 caused a flood of fortune seekers, known as "forty-niners." In less than a year, more than fifty thousand people poured into the San Francisco Bay area, lured by the prospect of striking it rich.[186] The government needed troops to help deal with the ongoing problem of newly arriving settlers colliding with Native Americans. Forts were established to help protect Americans and, in some cases, the Native Americans.

In their four years together, John and Georgie Adams had traveled the hot and dusty Santa Fe Trail, seen the distant snow-covered mountains of New Mexico, endured harsh Minnesota winters and watched the sun rise over the Atlantic. Now they found themselves in California, the path to their next post blocked by mountainous snow drifts. They were forced to wait at Red Bluff, California, from December 27, 1858, until January 13, 1859, when workers finally opened a trail through the deep snow.[187]

San Francisco in 1856, just a few years before John Adams and his family arrived. *Library of Congress.*

Fort Crook is approximately three hundred miles north and east of San Francisco in the Fall River Valley. It was established to protect travelers on the Shasta-Yreka Road. The buildings at the fort were made of logs, and the site was dotted with tall pine trees. In the distance, majestic Soldier Mountain stretches more than five thousand feet toward the sky.[188] Upon arrival at the fort, Adams conducted an inspection of the grounds and found the soldiers' quarters to be suitable. The officers' quarters were not. In fact, the building for the officers was not even complete. He had work to do. Arranging for and overseeing work at the post was not his only concern. Adams had had many dealings with Indians and settlers over the years, and once at Fort Crook, it did not take the experienced captain long to gain an understanding of what was going on in this area. One of his first letters from this new post asked the Department of California to clarify the boundaries of Fort Crook because "undesirables," as he called them (squatters), were already beginning to move close by. The Indians were peaceful at this point, but that would soon change.[189]

Adams noted:

> *With regard to the Indians in this valley, about 675, furnished with half rations of flour and beef. They seem to be perfectly satisfied and happy. I*

> *would venture to add, were the same number upon an Indian Reservation, they would be less content, and cost the Government perhaps $300,000. There are still a great number who have not consented to come near the Post. This I think is principally through fear of the whites settled in the valley. I regret to report that there seems to prevail among the majority of white men in the valley and on the road to Red Bluff a decided feeling of hostility against the Indians, so great as to render it very dangerous for the Indians to go any distance from the Post.*[190]

The supply problems at this new post included not having enough paper to write reports. In March 1859, Adams apologized for the "half sheet" he used for his report.[191] Adams fired off another letter expressing his frustration with the conditions at Fort Crook: "If there is a Post in the Department more in want of these extras than another, this must be it." He used a half sheet for this letter as well.[192] In addition to problems with the local Indians and settlers, Adams had to deal with deserters. He displayed his pragmatic nature in a report sent out regarding the capture of several of the runaway soldiers. He suggested the men, after they paid for their apprehensions, be restored to duty without trial. In the case of another captured deserter, Adams admitted he did not know how the man should be handled. Adams wrote:

> *I am at a loss to know whether he should be assigned to one of the Companies at this Post. In fact were there a Medical Officer at this Post, I do not doubt but that the man would be discharged as an Idiot, he certainly bears every distinguishing mark. Every day that he remains in service is a loss to the Government. I would most respectfully* [recommend] *that he be discharged.*[193]

As bad as the conditions were at the fort for the American soldiers, the situation was worse for the Native Americans who lived in the area and had tried to remain peaceful. Adams wrote prophetically in May 1859, "I am at a loss to say how they will subsist themselves next winter without the assistance of this Post, or robbing the Citizens of this and the neighboring valley."[194] In June, Adams sent a detachment to pursue and capture Indians who had murdered a white settler the previous winter. Adams did not want unnecessary bloodshed, and the outlaw Indians were taken without firing a shot. Adams noted, "I think that I may safely report the various tribes within this district are at peace with the Whites and desirous of remaining so. The fact of soldiers having gone among them, selecting these murderers without harming others, has been of great benefit."[195]

Even as the possibility of armed conflict grew, Adams wrote to the superintendent of Indian Affairs:

> *I would call your attention to the condition of the Indians in this and the neighboring valleys. They are numerous and at present probably as peaceably disposed as those of any district in the State, but white men are now occupying with thousands of cattle the localities best adapted and from which these Indians formerly dug the greater part of their subsistence. Other whites occupy the localities best adapted for their fisheries, nor will they permit the Indians to fish near them, in fact several Indians have been murdered within the past two years by them.*[196]

Adams suggested establishing a reservation in the valley where he could protect the natives from the locals. Should it be deemed advisable to establish a reserve for the Indians, "I know no place better suited than this valley. The whites acknowledge it is the poorest country in the State, they only live here to supply the Post with hay and others to annoy us by establishing whiskey shops on the boundary of the reserve."[197]

Finally, the Indians could take no more. They began by stealing cattle and harassing travelers on the emigrant road. In August 1859, Indians killed two white men. In response, Adams sent out a search party to find the murderers.[198] Adams moved men around the territory to deal with continuing Indian activities. In the meantime, a group of local volunteers attacked a band of friendly Indians on the nearby Pit River. Adams then had to dispatch men to patrol the emigrant road to protect travelers along that route. Adams wrote to headquarters to make everyone aware of what was happening and how the volunteers had turned a bad situation into a potentially explosive one.[199] Adams expressed his concerns to Major W.W. Mackall, assistant adjutant general of the United States: "I fear this on strong grounds for apprehending a general war with them."[200]

Other longtime settlers were disgusted at the massacre carried out by the armed civilians, and the influence of those citizens helped rein in the killers. Adams noted this in his report to Mackall in September: "I was fearful that the self styled Volunteers would continue this murderous attack upon the friendly Indians in the valley, but their butchering of women and children, being so unfavorably received by the public, has discouraged them, in fact, led to a division and consequent disbanding of the greater portion."[201]

Reinforcements arrived in the form of another group of citizen-soldiers from the state of California and a detachment from the Sixth U.S. Infantry. Things calmed down until October, when the volunteers murdered more friendly Indians and burned the grass and seeds the natives had laid up for winter. Adams again appealed for help because these armed civilians were not under the jurisdiction of the military. Adams expressed his disgust with their actions: "By their acts they are drilling the Indians admirably, and may succeed in rendering a tribe heretofore cowardly and harmless, quite formidable."[202]

Winter came, and the operations ceased.[203] Reflecting on the previous summer and fall, and in particular the role the volunteers had played, Adams wrote that before the volunteers came "everything like depredations or murder (except that of Indian women and children by the whites) had ceased, and such disposition of the troops from this Post were made and have been confined up to the present as alone prevented a recurrence of them."[204] Into these bleak conditions, on December 16, 1859, John and Georgie Adams welcomed their fourth child, Francis Joseph Adams.[205]

The new year brought more reports of Indian troubles as Paiutes from Utah joined with local tribes in California to conduct raids. Throughout the year of 1860, reinforcements from the state of California continued to arrive at Fort Crook, and the threat of an all-out war remained. Troops guarded the roads and fought the hostiles. Winter brought another lull. The new year of 1861 dawned, and as in previous years, snowfall blocked passes, supply issues arose and the constant threat of renewed violence lingered. Even so, Adams still managed to be thoughtful regarding the Native Americans. In March 1861, reports indicating trouble with the Hat Creek Band arrived at Fort Crook. Adams responded, "The white inhabitants of this section are more than anxious to be at war with these Indians. For this reason, the Indians are afraid to go into the valleys for roots and berries, so that I cannot imagine how they live, and must think they merit some consideration for not stealing."[206]

There was another, much larger, threat to the security of the entire country. As Adams dealt with the Indian troubles in and around Northern California, news reached the West that in April 1861, Southern men in Charleston, South Carolina, had fired on Federal Fort Sumter in Charleston Harbor. Southerners had long felt that their states' rights were threatened. The issue of the "peculiar institution" (slavery) hung over the ongoing debates. The election of Abraham Lincoln in the fall of 1860 hardened the resolve of those wanting to secede from the Union and start a new country, and by the time the first shots streaked across Charleston Harbor, some Southern states had already left the Union. Adams's native state, Tennessee, had not yet joined with the emerging Confederacy. Before the echoes of the booming guns that ringed Charleston Harbor had died away on the morning of April 14, 1861, and the projectiles slammed into the not-yet-completed Fort Sumter, the die was cast. There was no turning back. The nation was divided. The Southern men in the United States Army would have to make a decision: which country would they serve?

Adams's brothers and sisters lived in Tennessee. John Adams considered Tennessee to be his home. His now-deceased parents were first-generation immigrants and slave owners. His father-in-law and friend, Charles McDougall, continued to serve in the United States Army. McDougall was a staunch Union man and told Georgie's brother Tom on the eve of war, "My son, I'll stick to the United States, if only half a state remains."[207] The state of Tennessee remained in the Union until President Lincoln called for volunteers to put down the rebellion. The Volunteer State then decided to join with its Southern sister states, the last state to secede.

On April 18, 1861, Major George A.H. Blake was assigned to assume command of Fort Crook.[208] All officers were ordered to take the oath of allegiance in May.[209] On May 18, Order Number 7 came down from Headquarters, Department of the Pacific. Brigadier General "Bull Head" Sumner stated, "Any citizen in the employment of Army in this Department who is opposed to the Union will be instantly discharged."[210] That same day, Adams received orders to send Company E, Sixth Infantry, to Benicia Barracks in Benicia, California, "immediately."[211] The "Organization of Troops in the Department of the Pacific" dated June 30, 1861, still showed Captain John Adams at Fort Crook, California, commanding Company F, First U.S. Dragoons. His friend and former West Point roommate, Captain George Edward Pickett, was listed as commanding Company D of the Ninth U.S. Infantry at Camp Pickett, San Juan Island, Washington Territory.[212]

There are no existing records, diaries or memoirs indicating Captain Adams's thought process. We do know, from a review of his life and work up to this point, that he was thoughtful, sometimes questioned authority, was a good soldier, looked out for his men and that, whenever possible, he chose to use reason instead of force. We know that many of his requests for better food and equipment and horses for his men and for leaves of absence for himself to deal with personal illnesses were denied or simply ignored. The government had recognized him for his service in Mexico and New Mexico and promoted him to captain. Further advancement in the service of the United States, particularly with the coming conflict, seemed not unlikely. His friend Cave Couts left the dragoons and military altogether in 1851, married a young lady from a prominent San Diego family and settled in California. Couts seems unlikely to have influenced Adams because Couts sat out the war, living very well on his ranch in Southern California.[213] Maybe being replaced near the end by Major Blake had pushed Adams over. Perhaps being ordered to swear allegiance to a country he had served loyally all his adult life drove him to the conclusion that it was time to start over. Or maybe it was simply that his home state, Tennessee, was a Southern state and would likely join the rebellion. We may never know for sure.

On May 30, 1861, Captain John Adams, First Regiment United States Dragoons, sent his last dispatch from Fort Crook. There was no hint of anything to indicate he would be leaving soon.

Head Quarters Fort Crook
May 30th 1861

Major D.C. Buell
Asst Adjt General U.S.A.
San Francisco, Cal
Sir:
I have the honor to report that 1st Sergeant John Feilner, Company "F" 1st Dragoons, has been appointed 2d Lieutenant, 1st Dragoons, to date from April 23rd.

The appointment was enclosed to me in a letter from the Secretary of War, stating in case of his acceptance, he will report by letter to the Head Quarters of the Army in New York City.

Sergeant Feilner accepts the appointment, and will enclose the required oath to the Adjutant General.

As yet, it does not appear he has been assigned to any Company. Until further orders, I have assigned him to duty at this Post, there being no other line officer than myself here.

I hope the Commanding General may approve.

I remain Sir
Very Respectfully
Your Obedient Servant
John Adams
Captain 1st Dragoons
Commanding Post[214]

These two images are the same picture. The one on the right was taken when Adams was a United States officer; the one on the left shows a Confederate officer's uniform painted over the original. *Courtesy of the Tennessee State Museum.*

John Adams—native of Tennessee, son of immigrants, husband to a Northern girl, father of children born all over the country, loyal soldier for nearly fifteen years—decided to cast his lot with the fledgling Confederate States of America. Gathering his family and their possessions, Adams set off for New York City, intending to head from there to Richmond, Virginia, to offer his services to Confederate president Jefferson Davis. Leaving the service of the United States forever, John Adams decided to take one piece of public property with him when he left: his horse, Old Charley.

Chapter 16

Memphis

John Adams's resignation and subsequent travel caught the attention of President Lincoln's secretary of state, William Henry Seward, who sent a wire to the overall commander of the Federal armies, General Winfield Scott, advising Scott of Adams's imminent arrival in New York City via the steamship *Northern Light*. Scott replied to Seward on August 5, 1861: "I think it desirable that John Adams, a native of Tennessee, who recently resigned a captaincy in the U.S. First Regiment of Dragoons, be arrested and held a political prisoner, as I do not doubt that he designs to take service in the rebel army against us."[215] Adams arrived in New York and departed without incident.

An entry in the *Nashville Union and American* of Saturday, August 10, 1861, provides a clue as to how Adams likely eluded capture. The *Northern Light* steamed into New York Harbor on Friday, August 2, three full days before Scott's wire to Seward. According to the Nashville newspaper, John Adams returned to the city of Nashville on Wednesday (August 7) and proceeded to the St. Cloud Hotel.[216] He would have met friends and family there. This was a time of great excitement, as citizens and soldiers exchanged bits of news and rumors. The horrors of war had yet to hit the Volunteer State, so there was still an air of possibility. The dark days were in an unseen but not too distant future. Adams received word he was to report to Memphis, Tennessee, where he would be a captain of cavalry.[217] This was not a step up for Adams, as he had had the same rank in the U.S. Army at the time of his resignation, but the assignment to Memphis did allow for a family reunion.

John Adams brought his wife and children with him to Memphis, where his sister Martha was already living, having moved to the Bluff City after she married attorney Thomas Dillon Eldridge in 1854.[218]

As captain of cavalry, and commanding the post at Memphis, John Adams set up his headquarters in the Gayoso Hotel, across the street from the Mississippi River waterfront. Adams's excellent administrative abilities should have dovetailed nicely into his new assignment, but as he would soon learn, this conflict would be different in many ways. A fellow Tennessean, and soon-to-be-famous cavalryman, Nathan Bedford Forrest, is credited for a line that perhaps best summed up the way this conflict would be waged: "War means fightin' and fightin' means killin'."[219] This war would not reward negotiation and patience. It favored the bold and the ruthless. It would also rely heavily on citizen-soldiers, volunteers, and Adams had seen what volunteers were capable of in Mexico with the slaughter of the Mexican soldiers after the Battle of Santa Cruz de Rosales. He had just come from California, where the untrained, undisciplined armed mobs killed indiscriminately. Dragoon recruits may have started out as immigrants or drinkers or folks who had led troubled lives, but they developed into regular soldiers, subject to discipline and rules. On the frontier, lack of discipline and order could lead to disaster. This would be a new kind of war where old rules and ways did not always matter.

Adams did his best to get his post into shape, and he saw to the myriad details that needed attention. One of his duties was to process Federal prisoners of war. Memphis received many prisoners taken at the Battle of Belmont, which occurred in November 1861. At Belmont, Missouri, a United States force under an Illinoisan named Ulysses Simpson Grant clashed with Confederate forces under General Gideon Pillow, who was in turn under the command of the South's "Fighting Bishop," Major General Leonidas Polk, stationed across the river at Columbus, Kentucky. (Polk, an ordained Episcopal minister, was a friend of Jefferson Davis and cousin of former president James Polk. The "Fighting Bishop" moved to Maury County, Tennessee, before the war, and he and his three brothers built a little church where their four properties met. They named the church St. John's and handed it over to the Episcopal Church after the consecration. This church would one day catch the eye of an Irishman and fellow soldier named Patrick Cleburne.)[220] The battle at Belmont was inconclusive, and each side claimed victory, although the Confederates retained possession of the field. It was the first hint of things to come for Grant as he demonstrated his willingness to fight. During the battle, his troops were surrounded by

The Memphis waterfront along the Mississippi River. *Library of Congress.*

Confederates. His men wanted to surrender, but he told them that they had cut their way in to Belmont and now they would cut their way out. The Federal forces fought through the ring of Rebels and made their way back to their transport ships.[221]

United States prisoners of war from that battle arrived in Memphis on the ship *Ingomar*, which docked at the foot of Jefferson Street and unloaded its human cargo. Many of the Northern prisoners were German. Throughout the war, the Federal army would turn to German immigrants, or "Dutchmen" as they were called, to fight. The prisoners were sent on to Mosby's cotton shed at Second and Jefferson.[222] The owner soon protested "violently," so Adams, in an effort to be considerate, moved the men to another location, this one costing $30 per day to use. Adams, ever the administrator, suggested moving the Northerners to Baton Rouge, where, he reasoned, "they would be much more secure and less expensive."[223] This suggestion was not accepted, and within a couple of months, Adams reported that he had found and secured yet another location, a former "botanico-medical" college on Beale Street for $100 per month. A couple of Federal prisoners attempted to escape during the transfer but were apprehended and placed in irons.[224] One of the Northern prisoners taken at Belmont was Francis M. Smith, the servant of General Grant. Captain Adams was ordered to forward Mr. Smith to Columbus, Kentucky. From there, Smith was to be returned to Federal lines. Adams carried out the order on December 17, 1861.[225] As the number of prisoners grew, Adams continued to seek and find other locations to house them. He even contracted with locals to feed the prisoners.

On Monday, December 16, the Adams family welcomed a new member, baby Georgiana McDougall Adams.[226] Amid the joy of the birth and the activities surrounding his duties, Adams received a rebuke from headquarters about his returns, or reports: "Ordering Capt Adams to adopt such measures as will assure his ability to make complete and correct returns." Adams explained why he had not produced the reports:

> *My Post Return has been delayed with the hope to make it balance—it has been in progress since 30th Nov 1861. I am constrained to forward it now very incomplete. Nearly the entire Command are sick, left from Regts, Companies, or Detachments, I have not mentioned them by name, because it would make the return too lengthy. I find it impossible to balance the Return, from the nature of the different returns furnished here by the Commanders at their departure. The Citizen employees I have not returned, there are a great many in the Hospitals. The Quarter Master's Dept and the Commissary (?) they have not furnished me a list. Have received some orders and letters, a great many dispatches which are omitted. I have made requisition for Blank Post Returns, but have received none.*[227]

Apparently the Confederacy had a paper shortage as well.

In February 1862, Federal prisoners from the Battle of Fort Donelson began arriving in Memphis. Like Belmont, Donelson was a battle where the Federal troops were led by U.S. Grant. Unlike Belmont, this was an overwhelming victory for the North.[228] Grant would go on to greatness, eventually becoming president of the United States. He was born Hiram Ulysses Grant but changed his name to Ulysses Hiram Grant so his initials would not spell out H.U.G. He preferred to be called Hiram but became Ulysses Simpson Grant when his sponsoring congressman enrolled Grant at West Point under that name. U.S. Grant stuck. He graduated in 1843, so it is possible that he and Adams at least knew of each other from that time.[229] At Fort Donelson, Grant would earn a sobriquet: "Unconditional Surrender" Grant because of the terms (none but the unconditional surrender of the fort) he offered to his prewar friend, the Confederate commander of the fort, Simon Buckner.[230]

Adams lodged the Donelson prisoners in a house near the river and found a local supplier who fed the Federals at a cost of forty cents per day. Adams expressed concern for their lack of blankets and requested blankets be sent for the comfort of the Northerners.[231] Besides handling prisoners, Adams investigated reports of spying by Northern sympathizers. He also trained new soldiers, reported on forces passing through the city and supervised two hospitals, all the while carrying out the other duties required of a post commander, which included recruiting.[232] In those first days of the war, there was little problem recruiting. The problem was organizing these anxious would-be soldiers. Many men and boys, eager for adventure and a chance to get away from home for a while, rushed to sign up. Some of these volunteers turned out to be tremendous soldiers, such as Nathan Bedford Forrest. Some grew tired of the tedium of camp life and sought a way home at the first chance. Many of the Southern volunteers pouring into the city to join up even brought their own weapons. Others were unarmed. Some formed their own companies. All had to be processed at some point.[233]

The hospitals consumed more and more of Adams's time as the number of wounded and sick soldiers increased. In February 1862, after the fall of Forts Henry and Donelson, which opened up the middle part of Tennessee to attack, the medical stores were transferred from Memphis to Jackson, Mississippi, thus leaving Adams to his own devices to procure needed medicines for the growing number of sick and wounded.[234]

Chapter 17

"The Best Interests of the Service"

Up to the spring of 1862, Adams's commander was Leonidas Polk and Polk's commander was Kentuckian Albert Sidney Johnston. Johnston, a former high-ranking United States Army officer, had served with Adams in California. With the looming threat of a Federal army approaching from the North in 1862, the Confederacy reorganized its command structure in the western theater of war, and Adams's Memphis post was removed from the Army of Tennessee and placed under the Army of Mississippi and General Pierre Gustave Toutant Beauregard.[235] This was good news for Adams because the "Fighting Bishop" did not like Adams.

As early as November 1861, Polk was trying to get Adams out of Memphis. Polk wrote to Johnston, "I find there is strong reason for believing that Captain Adams is not filling his position as might be desired. His habits, I fear, are bad and this leads to other things not in keeping with the best interests of the service." The "Fighting Bishop" wanted Adams removed from Memphis, promoted to colonel of a regiment and placed in the field. Polk never detailed Adams's bad habits but later in the communication perhaps stated his true intention: "It so happens that we now have an opportunity of having his place filled by a person whom I know."[236] The person Polk was referring to was a man named "Colonel" L.V. Dixon. Dixon was part of a group that called itself the "Memphis Legion." Made up of businessmen, the "Legion" looked for ways to serve the Confederacy without actually having to fight, or leave Memphis, for that matter. Dixon and other leaders of the Legion sent a letter to Polk in August 1861, offering their services to Polk and the Confederacy. The Memphis Legion, according to these men, were "men of prominence and influence, who have large amounts invested in the commercial and manufacturing of this place and cannot leave [to serve in the army elsewhere] without great pecuniary sacrifice and, as we believe, without great inconvenience to the public." They believed it was necessary, if they were to continue to supply Memphis and the surrounding area, to stay in Memphis and not fight. Their letter stated, "Hence, it is, we think, important that as many of our enterprising merchants and manufacturers should remain at home and so arrange their military connections as to enable them to give a considerable portion of their time to business operations."[237] Polk indicated to Johnston that "this Legion is an old organization and one which I have been endeavoring to get to enlist for the local defense." Polk closed his letter to Johnston with this bit of news: "I have waived my resignation, as Davis seems very much opposed to it."[238] Johnston did not act on Polk's recommendations, and Adams stayed in Memphis.

Although he had made friends in the U.S. Army throughout the country, Adams now seems to have developed a penchant for angering some fellow Southerners. Along with Polk, another Confederate officer who was not enamored of John Adams was naval officer George Nichols Hollins. Born in 1799, Hollins was a navy man all his life. He served under Stephen Decatur during the War of 1812 and continued his service to the United States up to the Civil War, when he tendered his resignation. The United States officials refused to accept the resignation and tried to arrest him. Hollins offered his services to the new Confederate States of America.[239] George Hollins became aware of and immediately displeased with Captain John Adams over an order issued by General Beauregard for Adams to take eight guns from Hollins's naval boats and relocate them inland.

Captain Adams, trim and neat in his cavalry officer's uniform, strode across the street to the Mississippi River with his gang of gun movers, asked for and found the naval officer in charge, carried out his orders and took the cannons from the startled and likely angry sailors. When word reached Hollins, he became furious and fired off a letter to the Confederate secretary of the navy, Stephen Russell Mallory, on March 21, 1862. The old navy commander had sent a steamer to Memphis to collect those same guns to be sent to New Orleans. Hollins wrote, "I should have supposed the various evacuations of the Army had furnished navy guns enough to the enemy without those sent direct to my command for, perhaps the same purpose." After hearing that Adams had taken his guns, Hollins sent another naval officer to get the navy ordnance back. Adams refused and threatened to jail the sailors if they tried to get the guns. Hollins picks up the story: "I have the mortification of seeing my orders countermanded by inferiors and my officers threatened with imprisonment for attempting to carry them out." His fury building, the veteran of the War of 1812 concluded, "If I am to be subject to the orders of any and every officer of the Army, whatever his grade, who may be temporarily in command of any little post, my usefulness here will be of little avail in serving my country."[240]

Hollins did not resign, and Adams's time in Memphis was coming to an end. Hollins's letter to the secretary of the navy went out on March 21, 1862. Meanwhile, Albert Sidney Johnston, commanding the Confederate forces in the West, led his army up from Corinth, Mississippi, toward a large encampment of Federal forces set up around Pittsburg Landing, east of Memphis on the Tennessee River, near Savannah, Tennessee. Under pressure from Confederate higher-ups to be more aggressive, Johnston pushed his men into position to attack the sleeping United States troops. On April 6, 1862, the Kentuckian unleashed his green troops, and the howling Southerners tore through the first Federal camps they encountered. Startled, the Northerners fought to hold their positions but were overwhelmed by the determined Southerners. Some Federal troops fled all the way to the river, where their commander, U.S. Grant, did his best to keep order. Some United States commanders and soldiers continued to fight, including a determined group under Benjamin Prentiss who made a stand along a sunken road. This area would forever after be called the "Hornets' Nest" for the terrific fire the Federals poured into the attacking Confederates. Seeing his attacks stall, Johnston moved forward to personally lead his men as they struggled through a peach orchard, not far from a bloody pond and a Methodist church called Shiloh. Astride his horse, Fire Eater, Johnston disregarded the danger and directed his men forward until a Minié ball hit him in the back of the knee, severing an artery. In the excitement of the battle, his wound was not noticed at first. But the handsome Kentuckian began turning pale, and his fellow officers rushed to aid their commander. It was too late. Albert Sidney Johnston died on the field that day.[241] The Confederates did not recover from his loss. The gains of that first day of fighting were quickly swept away the next morning when General Grant, fueled by fresh troops, launched a massive counterattack. The seeming Confederate victory ended in defeat, and Johnston, a very capable commander, was gone. When news reached Confederate president Jefferson Davis of the death of Johnston, Davis noted, "My long and close friendship with this departed chieftain and patriot forbids me to trust myself in giving vent to the feelings which this intelligence has evoked. Without doing injustice to the living, it may safely be said that our loss is irreparable."[242]

A little more than two weeks later, on April 21, Adams reported to Corinth, Mississippi. His post in Memphis was handed over to General Earl Van Dorn. By May, Adams had received a promotion to colonel and was sent to North Alabama to take over a disparate group of Confederate cavalry in the field, just as Polk had desired.[243]

Chapter 18

"Our Regiment Will Not Move Under Him"

Adams's new command comprised scattered volunteer cavalry units. One of those was the First Kentucky (cavalry). Assembled in the Bluegrass State by Benjamin Hardin Helm, brother-in-law of United States president Abraham Lincoln, the horsemen of the First loved Helm, who was promoted in March to brigadier general and assigned command of the First Kentucky "Orphan" Brigade (infantry). After his departure, the Kentucky cavalrymen expected to elect their next commanding officer from among their ranks, as was the custom. Instead, General Beauregard assigned Adams to command.[244] This did not please the boys from the Bluegrass State.

Adams established his headquarters near Russellville, Alabama, just south of Florence and west of Huntsville. There was a recommendation before Confederate president Jefferson Davis to promote John Adams to brigadier general. In the meantime, however, Colonel John Adams did his best with the forces assigned to him.[245] Adams's command included the First's independent companies under Captains McAskill and Saunders and a regiment of Texas Rangers under the command of Colonel John Austin Wharton.[246] Wharton was the son of William Harris Wharton, one of the co-hosts of the Andrew Jackson party that John Adams's father, Thomas Patton, had participated in planning many years earlier. Now these sons of friends met up here in North Alabama, and things did not go well.

Wharton and his Texans were fighters. Adams was methodical. (A Mississippian would later describe Texans as "good in a fight, but...wild and reckless and troublesome, [and] hard to manage.")[247] Adams had demonstrated early on his concern for the welfare of his men when he was in the American Southwest. Wharton was a fighter who did not hesitate to use force. Their conflicting styles did not mesh here in the midst of this increasingly brutal civil war. It is not as though Adams kept his forces from fighting. There were skirmishes with Federal forces along the Elk River. There were casualties on both sides. In one scrap, Adams's men captured eight African Americans. Of them, he wrote, "The negroes I shall have tried by a military commission, and, if it is found that any were taken with arms in their hands, it may be necessary to inflict summary punishment; otherwise, I shall order them turned over to the civil authorities." There is no further mention of these men in the record. Based on his actions throughout his life, it is most likely that he turned the prisoners over to the civilian authorities.[248]

As in any war, both sides attempted to gather information on their opponents. During a lull in the frequent skirmishing, a man approached Adams's camp on horseback and claimed to be an escaped Confederate prisoner, making his way back south after fleeing his Northern captors. Adams began to question the man and ascertained that the lone horseman was lying and that his pass was forged. The man quickly tore up the pass, but it was too late. Adams had him arrested and sent on to headquarters for further questioning.[249]

Adams's cavalrymen wanted to fight, so he led his small force into Tennessee, intending to set a trap for Federals who were moving back and forth between Huntsville, Alabama, and Murfreesboro, Tennessee. Unbeknownst to Colonel Adams, however, Huntsville was at the time occupied by Federal major general Ormsby McKnight Mitchel and his force of upward of seven thousand men. Mitchel had also established outposts at every ferry on the Tennessee River and Elk River. Once he learned of these developments, Adams checked with Beauregard. The Creole assured the Tennessean he would send reinforcements.[250]

On May 9, 1862, Adams turned his attention and his forces to nearby Pulaski, Tennessee, where his sister Anne still lived. There were reports that Federal wagon trains were on the Pulaski-Elkton Turnpike. Colonel Adams left a portion of his force at Lamb's Ferry, south of Rogersville, Alabama, and took the remaining 850 troopers toward Pulaski and the wagon trains. Confederate scouts caught up to Adams and informed him that Pulaski was, in fact, occupied by 2,500 Federals. Adams then turned his contingent around and headed back south. Near Rogersville, Adams's group ran into United States forces under General James Scott Negley. The Federal force of 1,500 men included a battery of artillery. The Southerners had no artillery with them, so they formed a defensive position and waited all night for an attack that never came. The next morning, May 12, the butternuts discovered that Negley had moved on.[251] While Negley was moving, the Confederates at Lamb's Ferry departed for Tuscumbia, Alabama, with Adams's artillery and ammunition. Without these guns, Adams moved back into Tennessee. When they stopped near Winchester, Colonel Wharton advised Adams that he and his Texans wanted to form an independent company. The Tennessean agreed as long as Beauregard approved.[252]

The squabble over command likely arose because Wharton, who had been away from his Rangers while recovering from wounds received during an attack on Federal forces the previous month, expected to be placed in charge of all the cavalry units when he returned to active duty. Instead, he found himself reporting to Colonel Adams. This did not sit well with Wharton, who believed that he should be in command.[253] Adams said he would check with Richmond and Beauregard to get an answer and left camp to go to Chattanooga to confer with Confederate leadership there and wire Beauregard regarding Wharton's request. When Adams departed on May 19, Federal forces under James Negley moved into Winchester. Richmond did not reply, but Beauregard did with the terse response, "Date of commission determines rank." The beleaguered Tennessean returned to the encampment with this news and offered command to Wharton. A Texas Ranger, James T. Pettus, recorded Adams's return. Pettus noted, "Gen Adams rejoins the command but our Regiment will not move under him any longer."[254] Wharton refused the offer, took his men and left.[255]

(Wharton would rise to the rank of major general after distinguishing himself at the Battles of Murfreesboro and Chickamauga. However, he apparently never learned how to control his anger, and in April 1865, just days before Lee's surrender in the East, Wharton, then in Texas, insulted fellow officer Colonel George W. Baylor, whose own father had fought in the war for Texas Independence. Wharton and Baylor argued over an order given by Wharton. The two men were split up to cool down. Later that morning, they ran into each other again. Wharton rose to confront Baylor, waved his fist at the older gentleman and screamed, "Colonel Baylor, you have insulted me most grossly this morning!" Wharton then took a swing at Baylor, who responded by pulling out his gun and shooting Wharton dead on the spot. Baylor was never tried for the incident.)[256]

With the Texans now out of the picture, Adams set his sights on Fayetteville, Tennessee, and asked for reinforcements. On May 22, after Adams's return, Wharton sent a group into Winchester, and the Federals retreated.[257] General Beauregard sent orders to Adams directing him to Corinth, Mississippi, to take part in the defense of that city. As the colonel was moving in that direction, a courier reached Adams with word to remain in Tennessee. There was also a promise of reinforcements of two cavalry units and one artillery unit. Adams made camp at Sweeten's Cove, near Jasper, Tennessee.[258] If only that courier had not reached Adams…

Chapter 19

Sweeten's Cove and the Flying Rebels

Sweeten's Cove (usually spelled Sweedens Cove in the *Official Records*) is a narrow strip of land adjacent to Battle Creek, not far from Jasper, Tennessee. A Confederate described "Sweeden's Cove" in an official dispatch: "A valley three-quarters miles wide, six miles long, empties into Battle Creek."[259] The cove is very lovely, surrounded by hills, and the creek offers plenty of fresh water. It seemed to afford protection from marauding enemies, but the very narrowness of it would soon prove to be a trap.

Federal major general O.M. Mitchel had had it with guerrilla activity in the area. He wrote, "There is but one way of ridding the country of guerilla bands and that is to turn out against them a sufficient force of cavalry to pressure and utterly destroy them, with orders not to return until the work is done."[260] To that end, he dispatched James Negley to squash the threat posed by Confederates who were moving in and around southern middle Tennessee. On May 28, Negley's forces packed twelve days' worth of rations and moved south from their camp, toward Pulaski, Tennessee. Upon entering Pulaski, instead of continuing south to Rogersville as they had done several days before, they turned east and marched through Fayetteville and Winchester.[261]

Included in the Federal force were men of the Seventy-Ninth Pennsylvania Infantry. One of the Pennsylvania boys, Elias Witmer, recalled the march as "warm" and how the poorly fed and cared for United States horses panted and sometimes even fell as they plodded through mountainous terrain. Witmer felt sorry for the beasts but didn't mind the march itself. They

James Scott Negley of Pennsylvania routed Adams's forces at Sweeten's Cove. *Library of Congress.*

crossed one creek "forty-one times," and when they stopped they took a bath, ate supper and enjoyed a good night of sleep. Along the route, Witmer noted the poor conditions of the inhabitants of the region. There were no fine mansions here, just small log cabins and "illy cultivated fields." Continuing on, the contingent at last camped at the base of a spur of a mountain, near a passenger station of the Nashville and Chattanooga Railroad. Early the next morning, Wednesday, June 4, they began the climb up the western side of the mountain. Witmer found the climb steep, but once at the summit, he and the others were rewarded with a "grand" view. He described the water here as "good" and "abundant."[262]

The same day that the Federals were climbing the mountain, Adams's force, minus Wharton's Texans, and fatigued from having spent many days marching back and forth, huddled together in camp. The area was wet from recent heavy rains, and the Confederates were still waiting for promised supply wagons to arrive.[263] As the Federals began their descent down the eastern slope, word reached them that there were between six and eight hundred Confederates under the command of John Adams down in the valley, in Sweeten's Cove. Negley quickly formulated an attack plan and sent out skirmishers from Companies A, D and F of the Seventy-Ninth Pennsylvania.[264] Having just finished a forced march of twenty miles, Negley looked to seize on the chance to surprise the enemy. He positioned one section of artillery, the First Kentucky, on the Federal left and another section, from the First Ohio, on their right. The guns were "masked," meaning they were hidden from the enemy's view so the Confederates would not know what hit them until it was too late. Negley's men captured the Southern pickets and moved into the narrow little cove from the west. Around three o'clock on Wednesday afternoon, June 4, 1862, Negley launched his surprise attack.

James Negley, a native of Pennsylvania, was at his best this June day. His skirmishers moved forward. Colonel Adams, at last alert to the threat, drew up his cavalry in line of battle and prepared to attack the advancing Federals. Satisfied that his men were ready, Adams led his cavalry forward to drive away the enemy skirmishers. Then the masked artillery opened up. The startled Confederates reeled and tried to regroup, but as they were re-forming, the Fifth Kentucky (Federal) Cavalry under Colonel Haggard and the Seventh Pennsylvania Cavalry under Major Wynkoop rushed in, sabers drawn, whooping and hollering as they charged, and the rout was on. The stunned Confederates panicked. With artillery shells bursting among them and attacking infantry in front of them, the Southerners looked for the quickest way out of the cove. A Northerner recorded, "As the shot came thick and fast amongst them, they began to think about getting out of reach, and then our cavalry came rushing from the bushes and on them—and such getting away you never saw—they ran as if the devil was after them, dropping canteens, swords, sabres, guns, pistols, haversacks, overcoats." James Fields of the Seventy-Ninth Pennsylvania noted that when their artillery opened up, "we let drive and showered them in earnest from our cannon, which made them look two ways for Sunday."[265]

The Southerners poured out of the narrow valley, leaving behind their ammunition, commissary stores, clothing and weapons. Negley's escort, under the command of Lieutenants Wharton (no relation to the Texas Wharton) and Funk, plowed through the fleeing Confederates. The Fifth Kentucky and the Seventh Pennsylvania Cavalry picked up the trail and continued pursuing the Rebels as they struggled to make their way out of the trap. Negley attributed their escape to "the narrowness of the lane and very broken ground."[266] Adams attempted to keep order as his forces ran away and tried to rally them in nearby Jasper, but as Negley would report, "they cursed General Adams and rushed on with their foaming horses." They did not stop for anything or anyone, and they headed for the safety of Chattanooga, more than forty miles away.[267] The Federal cavalry chased the Confederates for five miles. A Northern participant recalled that the townsfolk of nearby Jasper "told us the rebels didn't run, they flew."[268]

In the aftermath, the victorious Federals counted twenty dead Confederates and around the same number wounded. They also captured twelve men, including two commissioned officers. The victorious troopers scooped up weapons, ammunition and other camp equipment left behind. Negley's forces lost two killed and seven wounded.[269] As word of the disaster made its way to Confederate authorities, the original reports stated that their killed and wounded equaled one hundred, including Adams and his brother.[270] Adams joined his routed forces in Chattanooga. Negley reported that Adams had escaped Sweeten's Cove and "the people of East Tennessee are wild with joy. They meet us along the roads by the hundreds."[271]

One possible explanation for how Negley was able to find and surprise Adams comes from a message from Judge Advocate General Joseph Holt, sent to Secretary of War Edwin McMasters Stanton. In the wire, Holt is relaying his concerns for two slaves who had escaped, assisted Federal troops and then were subsequently recaptured. Both of the slaves had come from southern middle Tennessee. One of the men had escaped from a Methodist minister at Sweeten's Cove who, Holt reported, "was with Adams' cavalry at the time they were driven out from that place." The other came from Fayetteville and had, according to Holt, "previously rendered valuable services to General Mitchel's command as he afterwards did Major-General Negley by furnishing them secret information."[272]

On June 9, orders came in for Adams, along with Colonels Scott and Wharton, to turn over their cavalry regiments to a rising Southern star, Colonel Nathan Bedford Forrest.[273] Humiliated, Adams did not shirk his duty and instead made his way, as ordered, to his new command.

Chapter 20

"All Prepared for Defense"

In July 1862, the Confederate command transferred John Adams to Columbus, Mississippi, some 140 miles northeast of Jackson and 60 miles south of Tupelo, near the Alabama border. At that time it was, for all intents and purposes, the middle of nowhere. Adams had been banished. The town served as a collection center for prisoners and a supply depot for other bases of operations. John Adams established his headquarters in downtown Columbus. This assignment did, however, allow the colonel to reunite not only with his family but also with his cousin Thomas Gibson.[274] Gibson, a native of Nashville, began the war as a volunteer serving in the First Tennessee Infantry. Captured after the fall of Fort Donelson in February 1862, Gibson was thereafter released, at which time he resigned due to ill health. He joined his cousin's staff in Columbus as aide-de-camp.[275]

Adams's duties in Columbus were mostly administrative, but one of the tasks was supplying the war effort with cartridges. Cartridges contained gunpowder and lead and were made of rolled paper that had been pre-soaked in potassium nitrate. (The potassium nitrate made the paper combustible.) The person making the cartridges rolled the pre-soaked paper and glued the edges of the paper together. The munitions maker then inserted a bullet in one end of the paper tube and tied or glued that end shut. A measured amount of gunpowder would be poured into the other end, and that end was then glued or tied down.[276]

To fire a cartridge, a soldier first set his rifled musket butt end on the ground, open barrel facing the sky. Then he tore open the back end of the cartridge. (In battle, he did this with his teeth.) Once opened, the powder would be emptied into the muzzle or barrel of the rifle. He then placed the bullet, pointed end out, in the barrel and rammed it into place with the ramrod.[277] To ignite the powder and fire the bullet down the rifle tube, the soldier had to place a percussion cap on the nipple of the gun, near the hammer mechanism. When the soldier pulled the trigger, the hammer smashed down onto the cap, producing a spark that ignited the powder in the barrel, causing an explosion that propelled the bullet out of the end of the rifle.[278] This is how both sides fought until the introduction of repeating rifles in the Northern arsenal.

Adams's faithful cousin Thomas Gibson served on the General's staff during the Civil War. *From* Battles and Sketches of the Army of Tennessee.

In August, Adams received orders for "all the troops at Columbus that can be spared from garrison duty to be moved" to Tupelo, Mississippi. The writer of the order, Thomas Lowndes Snead, Major General Sterling Price's chief of staff, told Adams that Price, "relying upon your well-known energy and experience, charges you with the duty of causing them to be transported without delay." (Price knew Adams from the Mexican War.) The orders arrived on Tuesday the fifth. The men were to be transported on Thursday the seventh. Snead indicated on the seventh that only two regiments were to remain in Columbus; the rest needed to be sent on to Tupelo.[279] A month later, Snead directed Adams "to put the troops which are still at Columbus in readiness to move at once." This order included "convalescents and stragglers."[280] The Confederate Army of the West was about to invade Kentucky, hoping not only to defeat any Federal army that stood against them but also to turn Kentucky to the side of the Southern cause. What the Confederates would soon learn is best summed up by a Southerner who, referring to Kentucky, noted, "Their hearts are evidently with us, but their blue-grass and fat cattle are against us."[281] The great scheme unraveled when Federal forces met and stopped General Braxton Bragg's invasion at Perryville, Kentucky, on October 8, 1862. After a fierce and bloody fight, the Confederates withdrew from Kentucky and fell back into Tennessee.

Initially, the victorious Federal forces did not pursue their beaten foe, leading the North to replace their cautious commander, Don Carlos Buell, with William Rosecrans, who did move the large United States force into the Volunteer State.[282] As the Confederates shifted to cover the retreat of their failed invasion force and protect Tennessee and the rest of the South, Adams continued to oversee the sending out of troops from Columbus. During the first part of November 1862, he was ordered to forward all the cavalry he could spare to protect the Mobile and Ohio Railroad. Adams's troops also performed reconnaissance to try to detect any movements of the Northern troops into Mississippi and also policed African Americans in the area, "restraining them and preventing their running about the country."[283] By the end of November, as Adams continued distributing cavalry and infantry, he found himself left with only a few hundred troops in Columbus.[284]

When not forwarding troops, Adams assigned scouting missions and pickets and organized army recruits. He oversaw work on earthworks and roads and stationed his pickets as far out as forty miles, setting up a system with couriers stationed every ten miles. Columbus soon would be thrust into the forefront because in November 1862, Federal movements set in motion a series of events that would culminate with the fall of Vicksburg, and John Adams would be thrown into the middle of the fight once more. General U.S. Grant moved into northern Mississippi in December and threatened not only Vicksburg but also Columbus. Adams's force in Columbus at this time numbered around six hundred men.[285]

In December, Adams notified his superior, Brigadier General Daniel Ruggles, who was in the state capital, Jackson, that two Federal columns, one from Corinth and the other from Oxford, had converged on Tupelo. Adams warned there was not enough ammunition in the Columbus arsenal and that he would need reinforcements and twenty thousand rounds of ammunition if his six hundred men were to hold the town against the reported three thousand Federal soldiers thought to be approaching. The quartermaster and commissary stores were still in Columbus. Ruggles forwarded the message on to Lieutenant General John Clifford Pemberton at his headquarters at Grenada and decided to attempt to send reinforcements.[286] Adams wired Ruggles on the seventeenth that Confederate cavalry under Colonel Clark R. Barteau were falling back without contesting Northern advances. The depots at Shannon and Okolona were destroyed. Adams asked for reinforcements, as he felt he could not hold Columbus without them. His message to Ruggles on the seventeenth included this plea: "Cannot you send the brigade to save Artesia? Otherwise we cannot get off the stores."[287]

Ruggles ordered the Fortieth Alabama from Jackson to Corinth. Adams received word on the seventeenth that the Federal onslaught had been stopped and that the Federals were falling back toward Tupelo. Adams wired Ruggles, "Enemy not nearer than Okolona. All prepared for defense."[288] He would never forget the lessons of Sweeten's Cove and would not be caught unprepared ever again. With the threat seemingly handled, in January 1863, Adams focused on the administrative side of his duties and once more sent a status report of troops stationed at Columbus. The report shows off Adams's eye for detail and offers insight into the state of readiness of the Confederacy in Mississippi at this point in the war.

Some of the troops had not yet been officially mustered into the service for the Confederacy but were still performing guard and other duties. The state troops, Adams believed, were drilled to a point of proficiency that would rival regulars of the same service time. One brigade was armed with .69-caliber muskets with altered percussion locks. A company of heavy artillery was stationed north of Columbus, but Adams reported, "they have no battery." Instead they had 30 percussion muskets, 10 Enfield Rifles, 4,000 thousand buck and ball cartridges, 5,000 musket caps, "two horses, two mules, and one wagon; all in good condition." Another company of heavy artillery, also north of Columbus on the Aberdeen Road, had 1 thirty-two-pounder siege gun, 1 3-inch rifle gun and 1 six-pounder smoothbore gun. A battalion of "Partisan Rangers" were stationed farther out, and they brought to bear 307 double-barrel shotguns, 320 sabers and 45 flint-lock pistols. A company of light artillery counted among its ordnance 5 six-pounders, 1 3.3-inch rifle gun, 400 spherical case and 500 solid shot, 80 canister and 200 3.3-inch rifle shot.[289]

The arsenal and its machinery were being disassembled and moved to Richmond, Virginia. Adams then detailed his defensive works protecting the city. He used the natural defenses of the Tombigbee and Looxapalila Rivers. He threw up a chain of rifle pits and breastworks and situated guns along the defenses to maximize effectiveness if attacked. He closed the detailed report by stating that the quartermaster and commissary stores were being moved to Jackson, per the orders of General Pemberton.[290] After spending months forwarding others, Adams received word on January 5, 1863, that Pemberton wanted Adams to move himself to Jackson and relieve Ruggles.[291]

Chapter 21

"The Vindication of a Man"

Jackson is approximately forty-five miles east of Vicksburg and was the main supplier to that vital river town. This was an important assignment, and while in Jackson, Adams received word that his promotion to brigadier general was confirmed, retroactive to December 29, 1862. His appointment had been delayed to investigate a report alleging that Adams was a drunk. It is possible that this is what Polk had been referring to when he wrote of Adams's "bad habits."[292]

J.D. Blair, of Columbus, wrote an angry letter to Lieutenant General John Clifford Pemberton on January 15, 1863, with a request to forward the letter to President Davis. Pennsylvania native Pemberton had sided with the Confederacy at the outbreak of war, at the insistence of his Virginia-born wife, and now found himself in charge of the defense of Mississippi and specifically Vicksburg.[293] Pemberton forwarded the letter. Blair demanded that Adams's nomination to brigadier general be defeated. Blair stated, "There is not a civilian, or military man here that believes he was capable of commanding this Post." Blair then reminded General Pemberton of Adams's "acts in East Tennessee when the officers of his Regiment gave him six hours to resign and leave." (Here he was apparently referring to Sweeten's Cove and the incident with Wharton.) Blair declared that Adams was "a devout worshipper of King Alcohol." In conclusion, Blair summed up his feelings: "Col. Adams cannot keep sober if he can get anything to make him otherwise. Go to the President and ask that this name be withdrawn or defeat it. Military officers here say he cannot command a regiment. Yours Truly, J.D. Blair."[294]

President Davis ordered an investigation. Several Columbus residents responded to the charges. All spoke favorably of Adams. Major W.J. Anderson knew both Adams and Blair. Anderson responded, "I have known Mr. Blair for many years, and have never for a moment questioned his integrity or veracity. I cannot therefore believe he would willfully make so gross a misrepresentation; I am consequently constrained to believe, that Mr. Blair has been deceived himself and imposed upon by some cowardly enemy of Col. Adams, who knowing the charges to be false, dared not make them himself."[295] Anderson, who had stayed as a guest in the Adamses' home in Columbus, made this statement regarding Adams's alleged drunkenness and incompetence: "I not only never saw him drunk, but do not remember a single occasion when I ever suspected him of being under the influence of liquor. With regard to the charge of incompetency, I say without hesitation that, in my opinion, there are but few Officers more thoroughly acquainted with the duties of a Post Commander, and none who could have discharged them with more promptitude and fidelity than Col. Adams."

E.E. Eggleston admitted that Adams would take a drink but "very temperately only," concluding, "as an officer I know of no objection to him. He always appeared attentive to his duties."[296] Isham Harrison had an office near Adams's headquarters and saw Adams "on the street almost every day, and frequently several times a day." Harrison knew of no problems with Adams. James Whitfield called on Adams at Adams's home and at his office. Whitfield "never saw him drunk" or "take a drink." George Clayton saw Adams often and said, "He always appeared interested and engaged with his official responsibilities." Thomas Christian stated, "I never had any intimate acquaintance with him, and consequently cannot be charged with special partiality for him, and only make this statement to correct what I believe to be an error."

Joseph Eggleston Johnston recognized Adams's abilities and wanted to make sure of his promotion to brigadier general. *Library of Congress.*

But the Reverend Phil P. Neely, pastor of the Methodist Episcopal Church of Columbus, Mississippi, made the most eloquent defense of John Adams:

> *I take pleasure in stating that he was my near neighbor—that in addition to my intimacy in his family, I was frequently in his office, during business hours, in fact saw him, almost daily and never discovered the slightest evidence of intoxication. On the contrary, his prompt attention to business—his devotion to the duties of his office, never permitting the pleasures of social life, to take supremacy over duty, impressed me with the conviction, that he had but one purpose, and that purpose was, to serve his country, in this dark hour of her fortunes. I state these facts, with great cheerfulness and hope they may contribute somewhat to the vindication of a man, whom I esteem for his rare devotion to his official duties.*[297]

General Joseph E. Johnston even weighed in on the matter with a message in which he stated his concerns: "I am just moving west to endeavor to join General Pemberton. Brigadier General [John] Adams has reason to think that his appointment was not confirmed. I hope the apprehension is groundless. He is very valuable. Please inform me."[298] Adams was confirmed, although not until December 1863, "to rank from December 29, 1862." (In the same report to President Davis, John Wharton was promoted from brigadier general to major general.)[299]

Chapter 22

Two Contests Won

In Jackson, Brigadier General John Adams took command of the newly formed Fourth Military District in the Department of Mississippi and Eastern Louisiana under the overall command of Lieutenant General Pemberton. Per the department's returns of January 31, 1863, the First District, in Columbus, under Daniel Ruggles had 3,110 men. The Second District, headquartered in Vicksburg and commanded by Carter Stevenson, counted 38,889 men. The Third District under Franklin Gardner at Port Hudson, Louisiana, numbered 20,733. William Wing Loring's Division (not assigned to a particular location) reported 10,032 soldiers. Adams's Fourth Military District in Jackson accounted for 388 men, or 0.5 percent of the total in the department.[300] The expectations for Adams and his military district were spelled out in a January 31, 1863 wire from Assistant Adjutant General R.R. Waddy. The missive stated that Adams could requisition troops from time to time to "perform police and other duties within the limits of your military district."[301] Adams's district included only the First Mississippi Battalion (state troops) and Bolen's Kentucky cavalry company.[302]

Adams resumed familiar duties, including housing prisoners. He sought permission to house the Northern men in the local penitentiary. The request was denied, so he had to put them up in part of a bridge over the Pearl River. Additional prisoners were housed in tents.[303] Adams also dealt with smugglers. One of the North's grand strategies from the beginning of the war was the "Anaconda Plan," whereby Federal ships blockaded Southern ports to choke off goods coming into and out of the Confederacy. Because of the blockade, many goods became scarce and smugglers came into play. The blockade did not, could not, stop the flow of all goods, and what did get through could earn the profiteers huge sums of money. In March 1863, Adams's men apprehended smugglers en route to New Orleans from Memphis and seized $75,000 worth of goods. Adams turned the men over to the authorities.[304] In short order, Adams's Fourth Military District grew. By the end of February, he commanded 1,231 soldiers.[305] By the end of April, the total jumped to 2,403.[306]

One pleasant diversion from the stress of war and the ongoing threat of invasion occurred during February 1863. One of the regiments that would be added to Adams's command was the Fifteenth Mississippi, headed by Colonel Michael Farrell. The Fifteenth received a challenge from a Colonel Thompson of the Third Kentucky Infantry. Thompson claimed his Kentuckians were better at the manual of arms and drill movements. There being no immediate threat from Federal troops at that time, the Mississippians and Kentuckians reached an agreement whereby their regiments would meet and see who truly was better. The ladies of nearby Canton, Mississippi, proposed to present a fine silk flag to the winner of the contest. A participant described the weather as "excellent." Crowds of soldiers and civilians ringed the parade grounds. General Adams and his staff entered the arena from the west, followed closely by Colonel Farrell and his Fifteenth Mississippi boys. Their band was playing as they quickstepped into place. The Kentuckians entered from the east. There was a panel of three judges: one from Tennessee, one from Louisiana and one from Alabama. The spectators included Lieutenant General Leonidas Polk.

The Fifteenth started the proceedings and went through its drills. Michael Farrell, a brick mason before the war, was well loved by his men, who had given him his horse, Bullet. Then the Kentuckians responded with their

Flag donated by Thomas Gibson in 1907 and most likely the flag Michael Farrell received in Canton for winning the regimental drill contest. *Courtesy of the Tennessee State Museum.*

Martha Jones Gentry, the "beauty of Tennessee's capital," hosted a party for Confederate officers where she lost a bet to General Adams. *From* Confederate Veteran *magazine, May 1897.*

movements. This went back and forth for hours, and both regiments performed marvelously. However, Colonel Farrell's boys threw in some "fancy" movements not to be found in Hardee's tactics. These slick moves made the difference, and when the winner was announced, Mrs. Lattimer, from Canton, rode out and presented the silk flag to the victorious Fifteenth Mississippi. Farrell's horse, Bullet, performed one of his well-known tricks and "about faced" after Farrell accepted the flag. The Mississippians then immediately marched over in front of the Kentuckians and raised three cheers for Thompson and his men. Colonel Thompson was gracious in defeat.[307] On the march back to camp, the band of the Fifteenth played "Ben Bolt," "Annie Laurie" and "The Girl I Left Behind Me."[308] They would play these same songs on another field the following year.

Sometime during this period, John Adams attended a party with other Southern officers. Mrs. Martha Jones Gentry, known as "the beauty of Tennessee's capital," and her husband, fellow Tennessean and Confederate army surgeon Dr. Watson Meredith Gentry, hosted the event. Mrs. Gentry wore a lemon-colored dress with broad bands of deep pink and black silk plush. She danced with Confederate generals and was escorted to supper by John Adams. During their walk to the dining area, they passed by a large punchbowl. There was a red apple floating in the punch, and Adams turned to Mrs. Gentry and told her he could pick up that apple using just his fork. She told him she did not believe that was possible. He insisted it was and said he would bet his fine pair of leather gloves that he could do so. She accepted the wager and then proceeded to look on in amazement as Adams balanced the apple on the fork and smoothly lifted it from the punchbowl. Adams won the bet. The demure Mrs. Gentry did not say what he won for his efforts.[309]

Chapter 23

"We Are Evacuating Jackson"

Meanwhile, Federal troops under the command of General U.S. Grant were not idle. Grant determined to take Vicksburg, "the Gibraltar of the Confederacy," and shut off that portion of the Mississippi River. Grant knew that if Vicksburg fell, the Confederacy would be cut in half and river traffic along the Father of Waters would cease for the Southerners. Northern troops began moving into place. As Confederate scouts and spies reported Grant's movements, Pemberton became increasingly nervous and put Jackson, Mississippi, on alert.

The Federals were indeed prowling, and reports reached Adams of enemy activity east of the capital. On April 23, 1863, Adams led the Twenty-Sixth Mississippi and two companies of the Fifteenth Mississippi to investigate reports of the destruction at Morton Station. The remainder of the Fifteenth and the Point Coupee artillery were to follow as soon as they could get transport by rail. Adams camped at the small town of Lake, where word reached him that United States troops had been through Newton Station, ten miles away, and were on their way to Enterprise, south of Adams's position. The intelligence indicated there were large numbers of the enemy. Adams wired this information to Generals William Wing Loring, Joseph Eggleston Johnston and Simon Buckner and also copied Pemberton, who wanted Adams to return to Jackson. Before he could comply, Adams needed to wait for the remainder of his command, the Fifteenth Mississippi and his artillery.[310] The message to Buckner is the one that got Pemberton's attention. It read, "All is lost unless you can send a regiment or two to

Meridian. General Pemberton directs me to urge you to send."[311] Pemberton was outraged when he read his copy of this wire from Adams. He fired off a message to Adams: "You say in your dispatch to General Buckner 'all is lost, unless' &c. Correct it. I never authorized you to use such an expression."[312]

April 25 was a hectic day for the Tennessean. This is his report:

> *Five hundred Federals at Newton Station this morning at 2 o'clock, have certainly gone to Enterprise. Heavy firing heard in direction of Meridian this morning. One regiment of Confederates came from Meridian to Hickory Station without ammunition….My engine has just arrived; report another heavy column of cavalry advancing on Newton Station from Decatur, Miss, and going to Enterprise….Eleven small bridges burned between Newton and Meridian.*[313]

At three o'clock in the morning, Adams sent out a wire to Pemberton advising his commander that he had sent out dispatches with couriers. Adams had received word that three hundred enemy troops had left Newton Station headed for Enterprise. The telegraph operator in Jackson even got involved. He wired Pemberton: "Did you get a dispatch from General Adams dated 3 o'clock this morning? The courier being absent (delivering a message) I left it by his bedside with lighted candle near it." The dispatch was signed, "Operator."[314] The next day, trains from Meridian brought news that there were no other Northern troops there, but Adams's scouts returned to camp and reported that Federals, perhaps as many as eight hundred, were about fifteen miles south. Adams wanted to stay and contest the movements, but Pemberton, fearful of a movement against Vicksburg, ordered Adams back to Jackson.[315]

The Federal activity Adams's scouts discovered was what came to be known as Grierson's Raid. Former music teacher and Pennsylvania native Benjamin Grierson led 1,700 Federal cavalrymen south from the Tennessee border through central Mississippi, tearing up railroads and generally confusing Pemberton. Grant intended this move to screen his positioning of troops as a prelude to pounce first on Jackson and then Vicksburg. Grierson's highly successful distracting maneuver finally ended when he and his tired troopers reached Federal-held Baton Rouge, Louisiana.[316]

Pemberton knew Vicksburg must not fall, so he ordered men, food and supplies be forwarded to the Gibraltar of the Confederacy.[317] From Jackson, on May 3, Adams advised Pemberton that he had forwarded 125 men from the Twentieth Mississippi, Federal prisoners of war and their guards. All

Adams had left were 350 men and two pieces of artillery. He asked if those two pieces should be forwarded as well. Pemberton replied that Adams needed to retain the artillery because Pemberton intended to hold the capital and he would "make some entrenchments about Jackson."[318]

On May 8, Adams wired Pemberton that he was prepared to construct positions for sixteen guns with rifle pits. He planned to anchor the line on the Pearl River yet still only had the two artillery pieces. Mississippi governor John James Pettus offered two state pieces. Pemberton agreed to the offer, and Adams now had four artillery pieces for the state capital.[319] General J.V. Harris, with six hundred state troops, arrived in Jackson, but Pemberton ordered Adams to send Harris on to Vicksburg.[320] On May 9, Pemberton wired Governor Pettus that he expected to have ten thousand enemy troops descend on Jackson in a few days.[321] On May 11, Pemberton ordered Adams to forward all of Brigadier General States Rights Gist's troops. Adams responded that Gist's troops had yet to arrive.[322]

River traffic moving from New Orleans or points north would have to pass beneath the guns of Vicksburg. As long as Vicksburg held, the Southern nation was intact. If it fell, the trans-Mississippi areas, including Texas, would be cut off. Confederate president Jefferson Davis's concern grew to the point where he exchanged nervous messages with Pemberton. Davis concluded one of his messages, "We look anxiously and hopefully for the next intelligence of your campaign."[323]

On May 12, Adams advised Pemberton that General John Gregg had engaged a heavy force of the enemy. Adams expected General Joseph E. Johnston to arrive the next day.[324] Johnston did arrive and established his headquarters at the Bowman House. Johnston, badly wounded at the Battle of Seven Pines the previous year, had been ordered to command the Department of Tennessee and Mississippi.[325] From there, he would assemble an Army of Relief to assist in the defense of Vicksburg.[326]

Although Johnston was in Mississippi, Federal troops continued to strike Southern positions. After receiving another message from Davis where the president offered suggestions, Pemberton snapped back, "I appreciate all your kindness and will endeavor to profit by your advice. I think, however, but little reliance can be placed on the kind of assistance you refer to."[327] On May 13, Adams wired that Federal general James Birdseye McPherson was advancing on Jackson with thirty to forty thousand troops.[328] The following day, Adams advised Pemberton that Gregg had encountered four United States divisions under the command of Major General William Tecumseh Sherman. Gregg fell back to Jackson at 9:30 p.m.[329]

Adams warned approaching Confederate forces to stay away lest they get caught in the tightening Federal noose. One of the messages went to a former West Point classmate, Brigadier General Samuel Bell Maxey: "Halt! Don't come any farther. Fall back on your wagons, and don't come any farther up the road. Go in the direction of, or to, Port Hudson. We are evacuating Jackson."[330] Maxey did not believe the message until a second message, this one from Johnston himself, confirmed Adams's information.[331]

Johnston determined that Jackson could not be held and ordered the evacuation Adams referred to in the message to his old friend Maxey. Johnston ordered Adams to move to Canton with as much public property as he could take. What was left of the Confederate forces withdrew from Jackson on May 14, and Federal forces occupied Mississippi's capital city.[332]

Chapter 24

Mechanicsburg

Adams had performed well since his move to Mississippi. However, while Pemberton was ordering Adams and other commanders to chase Grierson, Grant had moved down the west side of the Mississippi River, crossed his troops to the east side well south of Vicksburg and attacked the Rebels at Port Gibson. With that victory, he was able to establish himself on the east side, the Vicksburg side, of the great Father of Waters.[333] Grant knew, however, he had a potential problem lurking out there in the Delta hinterlands: Joseph E. Johnston's Army of Relief. If Johnston and Pemberton could unite their small commands into one large command, Grant could be in trouble. The Federal commander figured that each Confederate army numbered around thirty or thirty-five thousand, and combined they would actually outnumber his own forces, so he began sending out forces along what the Northern command referred to as the "Mechanicsburg Corridor," a strip that Grant calculated Johnston would have to use to move his men into position to assist Pemberton.[334]

To protect this corridor, Federal troops moved along the Yazoo River, debarked and moved overland, probing. On May 25, Grant received intelligence indicating that Johnston had six to eight thousand men stationed at Mechanicsburg, a little more than thirty miles north and east of Vicksburg. The wary Northerner responded by sending an expeditionary force of twelve thousand men to investigate. In fact, the only Confederate soldiers in that area were scattered elements under the command of Brigadier General John Adams.[335]

On May 28, Adams's cavalry met up with the Federal expeditionary force. There was a sharp skirmish on the road to Kibbey's Ford, two miles southeast of Mechanicsburg.[336] Adams rode to the scene and, as soon as he saw the enemy, shouted orders for his men to attack.[337] There were just too many Federals, though, and Adams withdrew his men across the Big Black River. The aggressive nature of Adams's move caught the attention of Grant, who feared that a large Confederate force could be nearby and withdrew this first expedition.[338]

On June 4, a second Federal contingent made its way along the Yazoo River and landed at Satartia, bound for Mechanicsburg. Adams formed a line of battle just west of Mechanicsburg and waited for the Federal troops. The general watched as the blue-clad enemy moved toward his position.[339] Fighting began, and as his outnumbered men checked the Federal advance, an excited scout galloped up with news that more Federals had landed and were making their way toward the area, threatening to cut off the Confederates. Not wanting another Sweeten's Cove and knowing his cavalry could not hold out for long against this large infantry force in front, Adams deployed skirmishers and retired back toward Pritchard's Crossroads. Adams set up artillery outside town and fired shell and grape shot into the pursuing Federals, who took shelter in ditches and waited for their own artillery to arrive, which it did in the form of two twelve-pounders. The Confederates withdrew once the bigger Federal guns opened up. Federal cavalry attacked the Confederate rearguard. Adams had anticipated this move and had ordered fencing torn up and thrown down to act as a barrier. It worked for a while, but the more numerous Federals pressed on.[340] Adams suffered about fifty casualties, including killed, wounded and captured.[341] He noted that the United States troops were "burning mills, gins, corn, etc. taking all provisions from the citizens indiscriminately."[342]

The Federals soon thereafter evacuated Mechanicsburg, not due to the heroic efforts of Adams and his troopers but because the Yazoo River level was dropping rapidly and the Northern troops needed to get out while they could. The Yankees torched Mechanicsburg on their way out of town for good measure.[343] On the march back to their river transports on June 6, many of the Northerners suffered from the intense heat and discarded equipment along the route.[344]

On June 8, 1863, General Johnston issued orders that outpost duties of the army would be performed by General Jackson's and Wirt Adams's cavalry. John Adams's mounted infantry were ordered to turn over their horses. After complying with these orders, Adams's men returned to their brigades. John Adams was ordered to Benton, Mississippi, to join the division of William Wing Loring and assume command of a brigade formerly commanded by Brigadier General Lloyd Tilghman.[345] Tilghman had been well liked by his troops, whom he was gallantly leading when he was killed during the ongoing Vicksburg campaign at the Battle of Champion Hill or Baker's Creek.

Chapter 25

A New Beginning

Adams's new brigade numbered 3,638 men. It comprised the First Confederate Battalion (commanded by Lieutenant Colonel G.H. Forney), the Sixth Mississippi (commanded by Colonel Robert Gadden Haynes Lowry), the Fourteenth Mississippi (under the command of Lieutenant Colonel Washington L. Doss), the Fifteenth Mississippi (commanded by Colonel Michael Farrell), the Twentieth Mississippi (under Lieutenant Colonel W.N. Brown), the Twenty-Third Mississippi (under Major G.W.B. Garrett), the Twenty-Sixth Mississippi (under Lieutenant Colonel F.M. Boone) and the Lookout (Tennessee) Artillery, commanded by Captain Robert L. Barry.[346]

When word reached the Mississippians that their new commander was not one of their own, they were not happy. They believed their new brigade commander should come from their ranks. Unlike the hornets' nest he walked into in Middle Tennessee the previous spring, Adams had just commanded some of these same men, such as the Fifteenth and Twentieth Mississippi, in the actions in and around Jackson. Major Walter Rorer of the Twentieth, for example, had spearheaded the initial assaults against oncoming Federals in May outside Mechanicsburg. Rorer noticed that Adams was doing what he could to improve the brigade and wrote to his cousin, "Gen. Adams, our Brigadier, seems determined to rid his brigade of incompetent officers. He is ordering them all before boards for examination but it seems a hopeless task. I have been engaged in this duty for three months almost constantly and occasionally for twelve months and as fast as we turn out one fool they send us a bigger one."[347]

John Adams's coat, worn in Mississippi and Georgia, now at the Tennessee State Museum. Length from top of collar to bottom of coat is thirty-eight inches. *Courtesy of the Tennessee State Museum.*

Adams needed to win over his new soldiers, but he also needed to see his family, who had moved to North Alabama during the initial evacuations of Jackson. One of the children was very ill, and on August 1, 1863, while his brigade was camped near Forest, Mississippi, Adams petitioned for a leave to go visit his family. His wife, Georgie, was pregnant with their sixth child. (Emma Portis Adams would be born on October 12, 1863, in Cahaba, Alabama.)[348] The leave was granted, and John Adams traveled to Alabama to see his family, see his sick child (who did recover) and make arrangements for a more secure location for them to live as well. He returned to his troops but asked for and received a second leave in November because his child had yet to recover at that point.[349]

Adams's brigade saw no action during this period but did move around quite a bit. They were sent to Newton, then Meridian, then Brandon, then to Canton, where they remained until February of the following year. From Canton, the Mississippians were then moved east, to Demopolis, Alabama, and then on to Montevallo, Alabama, in April. Always interested in the welfare of his men, Adams noted during this time that his men were "comfortably clad and well fixed."[350]

Chapter 26

Joining the Atlanta Campaign

Robert E. Lee's invasion of the North was turned back with his loss at Gettysburg on July 3, 1863. Vicksburg fell on July 4, 1863. These were dark days for the Southern Cause, but they still held Richmond, Virginia, and they still held Atlanta, Georgia. As 1864 approached, Lieutenant General U.S. Grant now commanded the United States armies. He devised a plan to advance against Richmond and Atlanta. Major General George Meade, the victor at Gettysburg, would move on Richmond. William Tecumseh Sherman would lead his army from Tennessee into Georgia. The two onslaughts were to begin in the spring of 1864.[351] Sherman would launch his armies, totaling nearly 100,000 men and 254 cannons, against Confederate Joseph E. Johnston's forces.

Sherman unleashed his assault on May 1, 1864, beginning the "Atlanta Campaign." As the Northern army moved south, Johnston knew he could not confront such a force in the open. He sought out strong defensive positions in order to conserve the most precious of all the resources of the South, its brave men, but these moves were not popular with the higher-ups when all over the map Confederate forces were falling back. One of the Southern commanders in the West with Johnston, a hard-fighting Kentuckian who had proven his bravery on the battlefield, John Bell Hood, did not favor this style. Hood advised another member of the Confederacy's leadership, Braxton Bragg, that if he (Hood) were in charge, "I am fond of large engagements and hope you will not forget me."[352]

Sherman continued his determined march south, with instructions to "move against Johnston's army, break it up."[353] Johnston contested the Federal advance, but each time the Southern commander took up a strong position, Sherman flanked, forcing Johnston to withdraw. Adams's brigade was sent to Resaca, some seventy miles north of Atlanta, on May 11 to join up with Johnston, who had withdrawn to that location.[354] As late as May 9, Johnston's chief of staff sent a wire indicating, "I do not think Resaca in any danger."[355] One of Johnston's problems was that he could not figure out exactly what Sherman was up to. On the morning of May 11, Sherman's forces appeared south of Dalton. Resaca was in danger now.[356] Adams's brigade arrived by rail around midnight and was thrown into the far right of the Confederate defensive line later that morning, positioned with Stewart's corps between the Wagon Road and the Western and Atlantic Railroad.[357] There was skirmishing throughout the day of May 13. Sherman launched an attack against the Confederate positions in an attempt to drive them away from the bridges across the Oostanaula River. Adams's brigade was in the front and helped stop several Federal attacks. Johnston countered by launching Hood against the Federal left. The attack was successful and drove the Federal forces back. Johnston intended to follow up with another attack on the morning of May 15, but word reached his headquarters that Sherman's forces were already putting pontoon bridges across the river near Calhoun, thus threatening Johnston's position, so the Southerners fell back once more.[358] As Adams's men fell back, they burned bridges in an attempt to slow down Sherman.[359] It did not stop the Federals, and Rome fell on May 17. Johnston took up a defensive position in the Allatoona Mountains.

As Johnston moved south, Loring's division, including John Adams's brigade, was placed in the rear, guarding the retreat. They were under constant pressure from advancing Federals. Sherman, always looking to flank, slipped around the Southerners and attacked at New Hope Church, to their south, on May 25. This fight continued into the first of June.[360] On June 14, the South's "Fighting Bishop," Leonidas Polk, Adams's detractor from the early days, died during the fight on Pine Mountain. Polk had joined two other commanders at the crest of the mountain in order to take a look at Sherman's positions and try to determine where to place their own troops to the best advantage. Unfortunately, this fine vantage point happened to be within range of Federal artillery, which spotted an attractive target: high-ranking Southern officers. A Federal shell exploded nearby, and most of the Southerners dashed for cover. Polk, however, stayed to get one last look. The next shell was a direct hit on the "Fighting Bishop," and he died instantly.[361]

In the ensuing battle, Adams's brigade continued to fight Sherman's juggernaut, and the Twentieth Mississippi bravely retook a lost position. This action cost the Mississippians more than 150 casualties, including their colonel, Walter Rorer, who was wounded in the attack.[362]

After Polk's death, General William Wing Loring temporarily took over Polk's corps until Lieutenant General Alexander Peter Stewart assumed command of that corps that included Adams and his Mississippians.[363] Johnston, meanwhile, withdrew to Kennesaw Mountain.[364] Sherman and Johnston probed each other's forces, always looking for opportunities. On June 25, John Bell Hood battled Federal "Fighting Joe" Hooker's corps, which had attacked Hood's position. Hood held his ground, and Hooker's attack was repulsed. The aggressive Hood then launched an unauthorized counterattack, which failed and cost the men in gray one thousand more casualties they could not afford.[365]

Brigadier General Adams's men were placed at the base of Kennesaw Mountain, on the extreme left of the Southern line with the brigades of Winfield Scott Featherston and Thomas Moore Scott. Up to this point in the campaign, Sherman had successfully maneuvered his way south. On June 27, he decided to launch a frontal assault. The morning began with a Federal artillery barrage that lasted almost an hour. Then, three Federal corps, attacking in formation seven lines deep, advanced on the Rebel defenses. The day was hot, and the smoke from the thousands of firing guns choked the humid Georgia air.[366] The Federals attacking Adams's, Featherston's and Scott's positions met a "galling" fire, and the three Southern brigades turned back the Federal attack on their position.[367] It was a lopsided victory for Johnston, as Sherman suffered nearly three thousand casualties compared to less than one thousand casualties for Johnston, but Sherman's supply trains still moved through the Allatoona Pass and Sherman could afford the losses. He pressed south, and Johnston fell back to Smyrna. From Smyrna, he fell back to the outskirts of Atlanta, having destroyed all the bridges across the Chattahoochee River before taking up his position.[368]

It was the abandonment of the Chattahoochee River defenses that may have been the last straw for Richmond regarding Johnston. Adams's men had continued to slug it out with the attackers, building fortifications and battling rain and mud as they moved south. The Federals would pound away at the Confederate positions with their cannons, but the Confederates remained in good spirits, confident in Johnston's strategy of moving, fortifying and making the attackers pay as dearly as possible before moving again to another favorable position.[369] Johnston's fortifications along the Chattahoochee, however, were considered very strong, and he gave them up without a fight. The Federals had slipped cavalry across the river on Johnston's flanks, and he felt that move rendered his line untenable, but that may not have been the case. Even Sherman later commented, saying Johnston's fortifications, designed by Francis Shoup, were "the best line of field intrenchments [*sic*] I have ever seen." Shoup, the designer of the works, later lamented that the abandonment of the works was "the final turning point in the fate of the Confederacy."[370]

Johnston may have done as well as anyone could have done, but it was not good enough for President Jefferson Davis, who had concerns about the general's willingness to fight as early as 1862 when Johnston, then in command of the Army of Northern Virginia, gave up Harpers Ferry without a fight and ended up on the outskirts of Richmond, at which point Davis wired his general, "If you will not give battle, I will appoint someone to command who will." Johnston did fight and ended up getting wounded at the Battle of Seven Pines. While he was recovering, the Army of Northern Virginia was turned over to the man who would lead those men to everlasting fame and glory, Robert E. Lee. Davis also believed that Johnston had not done enough

Battle of Kennesaw Mountain. *Library of Congress.*

to save Vicksburg. When an aide remarked that Vicksburg had fallen as a result of a lack of provisions, Davis replied, "Yes, from want of provisions inside, and a general outside who wouldn't fight."[371] Davis ordered Johnston to turn over his command to John Bell Hood on July 17.[372] One of Adams's men, Lieutenant William Harvey Berryhill, upon hearing that Johnston had been replaced, wrote, "It has cast a gloom over the whole army so far as I have been able to hear it spoken of. He [Johnston] was well beliked in this army. I do not know his offense."[373] Berryhill was not alone. Another soldier wrote to his wife, "Hood's the most unpopular Genl in the army & some of the troops are swearing they will not fight under him."[374]

President Davis struggled with the decision to put Hood in charge of the army in the West. He wired General Lee and asked for the advice of his trusted and well-respected commander. Lee responded that Hood was "very industrious on the battlefield, careless off." As late as July 16, Davis asked Johnston for his plans, and the beleaguered commander responded that he planned to turn over the defense of Atlanta to Georgia militia so the Army of Tennessee's "movements may be freer and wider." Reservations or not, Davis made the decision, and Hood assumed command.[375]

CHAPTER 27

THE FALL OF ATLANTA

Hood, now commanding the Army of Tennessee, decided to hold the Yankee advance at Peach Tree Creek, the last natural barrier between the Federal armies and Atlanta. He ordered Adams's corps commander, Alexander Peter Stewart, to contest Sherman's crossing of the creek. Stewart forwarded this order to his men:

> *By direction of General Hood you will cause the banks of Peach Tree Creek to be thoroughly examined in front of your division; place a strong skirmish line there, and cause the best defenses that can be made to be placed there. The object is to enable a small force to resist the enemy's crossing for some time. General Hood considers this of great importance, and Lieutenant General Stewart wishes you to give it your prompt attention.*
> *Respectfully,*
> *A.P. Stewart, General Commanding Corps.*[376]

Peach Tree Creek flows east to west about two miles south of Buckhead, Georgia, and three miles north of the 1864 northern limits of Atlanta. Sherman was bringing to bear James McPherson's Army of the Tennessee, John Schofield's Army of the Ohio and George Thomas's Army of the Cumberland. As the Federal juggernaut advanced, Southern scouts noticed a gap between Thomas and Schofield. Hood determined to attack the Northerners, but he would wait until they had gotten some of their men across the creek. Sherman guessed Hood would attack but did not know where. Federal commander Thomas reached Peach Tree Creek on July 18 and began crossing his forces.[377] On July 19, fighting erupted along the creek near Moore's Mill. Due to conflicting after-action reports, though, there remain some questions as to what actually occurred.

A.P. Stewart was Adams's corps commander at Franklin and wrote a moving tribute to him after the battle. *Library of Congress.*

The Confederates prepared for the inevitable Federal assault. Around one o'clock in the afternoon of the nineteenth, Brigadier General Daniel Harris Reynolds's Arkansas brigade was relieved by States Rights Gist's brigade and placed in position to cover Peach Tree Creek. Reynolds's force numbered 520 men, too small a force to guard this important sector, so they called upon a part of Adams's brigade, which had also just been relieved, to help fill out the line. Having done this, the men resumed their much-deserved resting. On the Federal side, Brigadier General Jefferson Columbus Davis ordered his men to fight their way across the creek and establish themselves on the farther shore. Around four o'clock in the afternoon, blue-clad troops from Ohio began pouring into the creek. They were followed by fellow midwesterners from Illinois. The Federal men overwhelmed the Arkansans stationed there. At that point, the 15th Mississippi under Colonel Farrell and two companies of the 6th Mississippi were ordered to rush into the mêlée and stop the advance. Farrell did not hesitate even though he knew his men had not had time to load their weapons. They charged straight in, weapons unloaded, clubbing as they went. The stunned Buckeyes stumbled back to the creek. Because of the boldness and swiftness of the attack, the Mississippians were now in the rear of the 85th Illinois, who, seeing butternuts between them and the creek, started to surrender before realizing how few men the Rebels had. More midwesterners, the 22nd Indiana and the 125th Illinois, rushed to aid their struggling countrymen, and Farrell was forced to withdraw with 52 prisoners. Meanwhile, Reynolds, a battle-tested commander, launched a counterattack that resulted in the capture of a few dozen more Federals and around one hundred guns. Reynolds's success was short-lived as more Federal troops arrived, and the fighting continued until dark.[378]

John Adams stated in his report that the Fifteenth Mississippi and two companies of the Sixth Mississippi regiments took part in a fight against advancing Federal troops. According to Adams, his Mississippians had moved forward to challenge attacking Federals. Their advance was to the left of the Confederate line. Adams reported that Farrell's Mississippians moved forward in "gallant style," recaptured lost ground and captured an entire Federal regiment. The gain was temporary because D.H. Reynolds's part of the line had not moved forward to support Farrell. According to Adams, other enemy troops moved to cut off the exposed Mississippians, who saw the attempt to ensnare them and double-timed it back to their own lines, leaving behind the recently captured Federal regiment. Adams blamed the loss on Reynolds and went on to state his fear that further Federal movements might be successful because Adams did not have enough men to hold.[379]

Reynolds heatedly responded that Adams's report contained several errors, which Reynolds attributed to the fact that Adams was not present during the fight. Reynolds claimed that it was *his* troops who actually advanced and that Farrell's stayed where they were, leaving his troops in trouble. Reynolds mocked the notion that Farrell's men had captured a regiment of Federal troops and then left them behind.[380]

Lieutenant Berryhill wrote to his wife on July 25, 1864, "Tuesday the 19th, the enemy crossed the creek above the mill and in the evening Reynold's Brigade and the Fifteenth Miss. of our brigade made an attack upon them. The Fifteenth made a gallant charge driving the Yankees before them and in to the creek, capturing and bringing off 52 prisoners. Some 200 or more surrendered to them but not being supported by Reynolds they all made their escape but the 52." This would confirm Adams's story. Near the end of the letter, however, Berryhill adds, "The fight took place two miles to the right of where our brigade was in line. Adams marched up to the scene of action but got in about the close of the fight and did not get to fire a gun."[381]

Lieutenant Berryhill had been placed in charge of the Pioneer Corps for Adams's brigade by John Adams himself. The Pioneers dug ditches, created fortifications and burned bridges. He liked Adams and the way Adams treated his men. He also liked the chances of the defenders of Atlanta. According to Berryhill, "We have the strongest fortifications here than we have had any where that I have been and I do not now think that Atlanta will be given up without we are whipped out of it, and I do not think that will be the case."[382]

The Federal army cut off Atlanta, severing the rail and communication lines. At the end of July, the Federals captured and destroyed many of the Confederate quartermaster wagons along with their precious supplies and the personal effects of many of the officers. Adams's brigade was just west of Atlanta. As the Federals began tightening the noose, morale fell in the ranks of the men in gray. Berryhill noted, "Our army are beginning to show some signs of demoralization and I hear of desertions occasionally. But I do not suppose that an army has ever stood up better than this. Gen. Johnston is still the favourite of this army and could lead them farther than any man living. Hood is a great Gen. but he cannot manage to keep up the spirit of the army as Johnston did."[383]

Hood's attacks along Peach Tree Creek in July had failed with heavy losses. In nine days, Hood's army lost twenty thousand men.[384] After unsuccessfully attempting to smash his way free, and finding himself nearly cut off by Federal troops encircling his army, Hood withdrew the Army of Tennessee from Atlanta. As the troops prepared to abandon the city, however, someone remembered, too late, that there were railcars full of munitions and supplies parked east of town. Somehow these eighty-one cars and five steam engines had been overlooked, and since the Federals controlled all the rail lines in and out of Atlanta, there was only one choice: blow them up. So, before departing, a crew went out to the Georgia Railroad line, near the Markham and Schofield Rolling Mill, and set fire to the rolling stock and engines. Six six-pounders; one three-inch rifled cannon; three twelve-pounder howitzers; many caissons, limbers and carriages; fourteen thousand artillery rounds; five thousand brand-new Enfield or Tower muskets; and countless other small arms, ammunition and implements of war were all put to the torch. In all, $6 million worth of ordnance and supplies were blown up that night.[385] General Lee's concerns regarding Hood's abilities off the battlefield proved to be quite accurate.

Adams's brigade departed at 10:00 p.m. and marched to Lovejoy Station. The fires from the explosions in Atlanta, Lieutenant Berryhill noted, made a light "so that we could see very well to travel five miles away."[386] Atlanta fell on September 2, 1864. Federal general Sherman wired Washington, D.C., on the third: "Atlanta is ours and fairly won."[387]

Reflecting later on Hood's costly attacks along Peachtree Creek, a Texas private wrote, "We fought hard, lost heavily, and accomplished nothing."[388] Those words would prove to be eerily prophetic for another great battle that was looming for the Army of Tennessee.

Chapter 28

Hood Decides to Move North

After the fall of Atlanta, Hood moved around the great city, to the west and north, intent on striking Sherman's supply lines and drawing the Federals out to fight on ground Hood would choose. This strategy seemed to work for a few weeks until Sherman, weary of pursuing Hood, made up his mind to turn his great Northern hordes to the east, to the sea, and lay waste to everything in his path and make Georgia "howl." Stymied in his attempts to draw Sherman into a fight, Hood made up his mind to move north, back through Tennessee and on to the Ohio River.[389]

Adams's brigade often found itself at or near the front of the advance. Near Acworth, Georgia, Adams's brigade encountered a two-story brick house fronted by a large, open field and a ditch eight feet wide and six feet deep. This imposing structure was manned by an unknown number of Federal soldiers. Adams drew up his men and placed the Fifteenth Mississippi in front and sent a member of his staff, Major Patrick Henry, to demand the surrender of the blockhouse.

Adams rode up to Colonel James R. Binford, of the Fifteenth and told him, "If they refuse [to surrender], I want you to charge and take that brick house they occupy." Binford said he "thought (in my wicked heart) it was h---, but that I would do it." After Adams rode away, the colonel silently fretted over whether or not, given the ditch and other dangers known and unknown associated with the possible storming, he really could take the house. Fortunately, the Federals surrendered, and without having fired a single shot, 236 enemy soldiers, their weapons and other supplies fell into the arms of the waiting Southerners. Adams allowed that, since Binford's Mississippians had been ready to attack, they should be the ones to receive the prisoners. The Fifteenth also appropriated the Federal supplies. Binford later recalled, "We were hungry and wet, and enjoyed the sutler's supplies greatly, which included substantial refreshments."[390]

On these marches, Adams demonstrated that he was worthy of the men's loyalty. Major Henry noted that the men learned that he was a

> *fine soldier, a knightly commander, and a Christian gentleman….I want to say that he was not only one of the bravest but one of the most conscientious and truly religious men I ever knew. He was as modest as a woman, rather retiring in his disposition, of the strictest integrity. He scorned that which was not honorable, and lived in daily communion with his God. I rarely ever knew him to lie down at night that he did not read from his rubric and say his prayers. This was often beset with difficulties on forced marches, but "Billie," his faithful servant, generally had a piece of candle stuck in a bayonet or a torch close to the General's pallet or blanket. There was nothing of the fanatic about him, nor did he make parade of his religion; he simply worshipped his God. Even now the old men of his brigade speak his name in reverence and affection, and as a token of my veneration for him I write these memories.*[391]

Hood pushed his Army of Tennessee into Alabama and sought a place to cross the Tennessee River. He intended to cross at Decatur, but the Federal garrison there, backed by gunboats in the river, foiled his plans. He moved west again, this time to Tuscumbia, Alabama, intending to cross at Florence.[392] At last he found a crossing place. Here, he would bring up his massive pontoon bridges. Here, he would watch as his men crossed the river. And here he would dream of the victory that he would achieve. It was a bold plan, and the Confederacy needed bold plans now. This would be its last chance in the West.

Chapter 29

Adams's Brigade

For this last, best hope, the Confederates prepared to move into Tennessee. Hood's army was divided into three corps. Each of these corps consisted of three divisions. Divisions were typically made up of two to four brigades that were commanded by brigadier generals. A brigade normally contained four regiments, each with 1,000 men; at the beginning of the war, this would have meant a brigade could have had about 4,000 soldiers.[393] However, by the time of the Battle of Franklin, the units and regiments were much depleted. Adams's division commander was Major General William Wing Loring. The corps commander was Lieutenant General Alexander Peter Stewart. Adams's brigade consisted of the Sixth, Fourteenth, Fifteenth, Twentieth, Twenty-Third and Forty-Third Mississippi regiments.[394] In theory, a division could have 8,000 to 16,000 men. The total number of men in Loring's Division going into Tennessee was a little more than 3,400.[395]

These six Mississippi regiments came from all across the Magnolia State. One company of the Twentieth hailed from Harrison County, on the Gulf Coast. Companies of the Twenty-Third came from as far north as Tippah and Tishomingo Counties. There were men from Coahoma County on the Mississippi River and Monroe County on the Alabama border. They were soldiers who seldom knew victory yet continued to fight hard, whether battling Federals, the elements, hunger or disease. General George Crittenden, praising the Fifteenth Mississippi for its heroic fighting at Fishing Creek, wrote what could be the epitaph for Adams's brigade when he stated, "The reputation of the Mississippians for heroism was fully sustained by this regiment."[396] Paraphrasing the poet Rupert Brooke, there are parts of many distant fields that are forever Mississippi, because these regiments buried their dead as far north as Chicago, Illinois, as far south as the Gulf Coast, as far east as Virginia and as far west as Louisiana. Some surrendered at Fort Donelson, some at Vicksburg, all of them had marched away from a burning Atlanta. They had fought in those well-known battles and others, less well known, such as Coffeeville, Lickskillet Road and Corinth. But they were still ready to fight and die for their country.

SIXTH MISSISSIPPI

The Sixth mustered into service in Grenada, Mississippi, in August 1861. The regiment's number changed to the Seventh until November, when its designation reverted back to the Sixth. The various companies picked their own nicknames, and the Sixth included the "Rankin Rough and Readies," the "Rockport Steel Blades" and the "Simpson Fencibles." At the beginning of the war, they were sent to Kentucky, where they suffered terribly from the measles and typhoid fever. The Sixth fought at Shiloh under the famed Irish Confederate Patrick Cleburne. The Mississippians attacked a Federal camp and withstood withering fire, suffering 300 killed and wounded out of the 425 men who entered the fight. Cleburne, writing about the Sixth after the battle, noted, "It would be useless to enlarge on the courage and devotion of the Sixth Mississippi. The facts as recorded speak louder than any words of mine." They later fought at Corinth, Port Gibson and in the Atlanta Campaign at Resaca, New Hope Church and Lickskillet Road (Ezra Church). The Sixth was also called on to deal with troublemakers in Jones County, Mississippi, by rounding up deserters and dealing with armed men who were "terrorizing local inhabitants." Going into Tennessee with Adams, they were commanded by Colonel Robert Gadden Haynes Lowry. Lowry had assumed temporary command of the entire brigade when Adams had taken his leave the previous fall.[397]

FOURTEENTH MISSISSIPPI

Mustered into service in Corinth in May 1861, the Fourteenth counted among its number the "Shubuta Rifles," the "Meridian Invincibles" and the "Columbus Riflemen." They had been destined for the disastrous Battle of Mill Springs or Fishing Creek, where Confederate brigadier general Felix

Kirk Zollicoffer earned the distinction of being one of the first Confederate generals killed in battle, but a change in command spared them. They fought at Fort Donelson, Coffeeville and in the Vicksburg and Atlanta Campaigns. At Fort Donelson, they charged a Federal battery for an hour before being ordered to retire. At Coffeeville, Mississippi, they engaged the advance guard of Grant's forces, thwarting his plans. Colonel Washington L. Doss led the Fourteenth northward.[398]

Fifteenth Mississippi

The Fifteenth was formed at Corinth in May 1861. Michael Farrell's company, E, the "McClung Rifles," came from Duck Hill in Carroll County. Other companies that mustered in at Corinth included the "Winona Stars," "Oktibbeha Plough Boys" and the "Choctaw Greys." The Fifteenth fought at Fishing Creek, Shiloh, Baton Rouge, Cypress Creek (outside Corinth), Coffeeville and in the Vicksburg and Atlanta Campaigns. The Fifteenth's actions at Fishing Creek likely saved the main part of the Confederate army there from capture. At Shiloh, they helped capture Prentiss's division. At Corinth, they charged and took a Federal battery and drove the enemy from their trenches. Colonel Michael Farrell led the Fifteenth as they marched north.[399]

Twentieth Mississippi

Formed in Iuka in July 1861, the Twentieth had the distinction of serving under the great Robert E. Lee in Virginia, where in the Kanawha Valley and mountains of what is today West Virginia they suffered badly due to the weather and lack of adequate clothing, food and shelter. Many men died. From there, they were ordered to South Carolina. On their way to the Palmetto State, they were rerouted to Tennessee and then Kentucky, then back to Tennessee, where they manned the trenches at Fort Donelson. When it became obvious the fort would fall, the Twentieth planned to escape and went to the river, where they were to board boats that would take them to safety. What ended up happening was the Twentieth stood guard "like a stone wall," remembered Major Brown of the Twentieth, while Virginia troops of General John B. Floyd embarked on the boats and left the Mississippians to surrender. Exchanged, they reentered the service and fought against Federal gunboats at Greenwood, Mississippi. They also fought in the Vicksburg Campaign at Baker's Creek (Champion Hill) and the Atlanta Campaign. A fellow Confederate officer wrote his opinion of Walter Rorer and the Twentieth Mississippi: "The soldierly qualities of Major Rorer, his officers and men, never complaining, always ready for duty and anxious to meet and punish the foe, won my admiration." Colonel William Brown commanded the Twentieth entering Tennessee.[400]

TWENTY-THIRD MISSISSIPPI

Mustered in at Iuka in August 1861 as the Second Mississippi, the "Tippah Tigers," "Blackland Gideonites" and "Plentitude Invincibles" and the rest of the regiment went first to Virginia and then were ordered to Kentucky as the Third Mississippi. Many of the men became sick and died from typhoid fever and the measles. They fought at Fort Donelson, where they surrendered as ordered. The more than five hundred men who surrendered were sent to Federal prison camps in Indianapolis, Indiana, and Camp Douglas in Chicago. More than ninety men died in those prisons. After the regiment was exchanged, they were re-formed and renamed the Twenty-Third. They fought in the Vicksburg and Atlanta Campaigns. At Coffeeville, the Twenty-Third earned the praise of Brigadier General Lloyd Tilghman, who wrote of their valor, "I have seldom seen greater good judgement and impetuous gallantry shown by any officers or men." Going into Tennessee, they were led by Major George W.B. Garrett.[401]

FORTY-THIRD MISSISSIPPI

They fought at Corinth and in the Vicksburg and Atlanta Campaigns. At Corinth in October 1862, the Forty-Third managed to break through the Federal lines and enter the heart of town. In May 1863, the Forty-Third met and repulsed a Federal assault on Graveyard Road outside Vicksburg. During the fighting east of Vicksburg, six men of the Forty-Third were digging a counter trench when a Federal mine exploded, burying and killing them. On May 29, 1864, Miss Helen Cozart of Columbus, Mississippi, presented a flag to "Col. Harrison and his gallant Forty-third as a slight token of the appreciation felt for the unflinching discharge of their duty in their country's defense." Colonel Richard Harrison led the Forty-Third into Tennessee.[402]

Chapter 30

Crossing the River

Sunday, November 20, 1864

Hood looked on as his army continued crossing the Tennessee River. It was cold, and a steady rain added to the misery of this passage. It seemed that even the weather conspired against him. His army had been trying to cross the river for nearly a week.[403] A.P. Stewart's corps finally began to cross on November 19. Lead elements stood and waited in the cold rain as the wagons struggled across the bridge.[404] The dull, whitish-gray sky blended into the horizon. Men could see their breath as they talked and breathed. Waiting their turn to march onto the wooden pontoon bridge, thousands of tired, hungry Confederate soldiers stared into the distance, trying to discern their future.

The pontoon bridge was a useful structure put together by teams of men, each specializing in various stages of the building process. The abutment crew prepared the approaches to the bridge on either side of the river, clearing away brush along the bank and leveling out the approaches to the water to build roads. As the abutment crew worked, the boat crew dragged heavy boats out of carrier wagons and began placing these boats in the water. Rowing upstream, they used anchor cables and set the pontoon boats in place, the sides of the pontoons being parallel to the shore. The balk crew placed wooden cross-ties or "balks" into place across the boats. These served as spacers and floor timbers for the deck that would soon be applied

A Civil War pontoon bridge. *Library of Congress.*

by the lashing crew who lashed the pieces together. All this work continued simultaneously until the job was completed. A chess crew covered the balks with the wooden flooring or deck of the bridge. The "chess" were the cross planks. The side rail crew then affixed side rails to the flooring to hold the chess in place.[405] Once all the pieces were assembled, other workers tightened the cables as the crews began walking the bridge, always on the lookout for floating debris or any other signs of trouble.[406]

Before moving across the bridge, Lieutenant Colonel Walter A. Rorer of the Twentieth Mississippi made a prediction: "I am going into Tennessee a lieutenant colonel but I will come out either a brigadier general or a corpse."[407] Not long before he crossed the river, he wrote a letter to his cousin that ended with these words: "When the war is over, there will be but few of us to return home. The list of our dead is terrible to contemplate, noble martyrs in a holy cause, for there is no cause more holy than the cause of our country."[408]

Chapter 31

The March to Redemption

The March Begins: Monday, November 21, 1864

Waking on the morning of November 21, the first thing the men noticed was how much colder it was. The bad, muddy, rutted roads had frozen overnight.[409] Wet and cold or icy and cold—either way it was miserable. General Hood issued a proclamation on this day that read, in part, "You march today to redeem by your valor one of the fairest portions of our Confederacy. This can only be achieved by battle and by victory."[410] After a quick, insufficient breakfast, the men formed into lines and began moving north. Stumbling along frozen roads, the march to redemption began in a snowstorm that started around ten o'clock in the morning. One of the Southerners noted, "Very cold with the wind from the north, wind and snow in our faces all day."[411] The brigade marched until after dark. They camped near a mill and used the planks for shelters and as fuel for large fires.[412]

Ice Formations: Tuesday, November 22, 1864

Another cold morning greeted the soldiers. Snow covered the ground. Rocks protruded through the sides of the hill next to the road. The trees were bare. The day broke bright and beautiful, but the snow started falling again around 11:00 a.m. and continued throughout the day, even when the sun was shining. The men noticed ice formations, some as long as six feet, stretching from the rocks toward the ground but not quite reaching. They crossed the Tennessee state line into Wayne County around sunset. Adams was back in his home state.[413]

DEALING WITH UNION TORIES: WEDNESDAY, NOVEMBER 23, 1864

Once in Tennessee, Stewart's corps, including Adams's brigade, split from the other two corps to march along a northeastern route toward the town of Lawrenceburg. Stephen Dill Lee's corps led the advance as they had crossed the bridge first. Lee's corps moved north, in the center of the advance, toward Henryville. Benjamin Franklin "Frank" Cheatham's corps was on the left, heading to Waynesboro.[414] Stewart's corps moved on the right of the Confederate advance. The road Adams and his brigade took from Florence continued uphill for some distance. The grade was slight, but to tired men (and horses), it was still a hill.[415]

Finally a day without snow! It was still very cold, and the ground was frozen, but the sun shone all day. The Mississippians began their march at sunrise toward Lawrenceburg, ten miles away. Men reported seeing ice one inch thick.[416] The bitter, wicked wind that had slashed at the men eased this day. Around midday, some of the top crust of the ice began to thaw, but it would refreeze that night.

There were many people in Wayne and Lawrence Counties loyal to the Union. The Confederates called them "Union Tories." They made it dangerous for individual soldiers to leave the camp to forage. But in the end, the hungry, cold Confederates went into the neighborhoods, taking what they could and destroying property as they went.[417]

OUT OF THE VALLEY: THURSDAY, NOVEMBER 24, 1864

The army rose and began to march at sunrise. There were no bread rations today, only meat. The day was cool and dark, but there would be no snow or bitter wind.[418] Lieutenant Berryhill noted that it was a "pleasant" day for walking "except the sloppy road" that was due to the ice melting and the ground turning into mud.[419] Stewart's corps turned west to join with the rest of the combined Army of Tennessee. United once more, the Southerners marched on to Mount Pleasant.[420]

Federal major general John McAllister Schofield's army and the food, weapons and equipment that went with it were the prize for the Southerners. The Federals had been in Pulaski, Tennessee, when Hood's army moved into the state. Alerted to the threat, Schofield put his army in motion, moving north to get to the protection of Nashville and the troops there, commanded by the "Rock of Chickamauga," the hard-fighting Virginian who had chosen to remain loyal to the United States, Major General George Henry Thomas. If Hood could get north of and trap Schofield's army, then maybe Hood could change the course of the war.

Adams's brigade marched up a creek valley. High hills on either side framed the path. There was one creek that the men crossed eighteen times, according to one of the Confederates. The narrow road at last came out on a large, good turnpike connecting Waynesboro to Columbia.[421]

CAMPING NEAR MOUNT PLEASANT: FRIDAY, NOVEMBER 25, 1864

Leaving at sunrise, the army moved along the turnpike and crossed the Buffalo River below Henryville.[422] They began to pick up the pace. The improving weather lifted the spirits of the men. Schofield had made it to Columbia ahead of the pursuing Confederates, despite the efforts of Nathan Bedford Forrest's cavalry. The day was mostly clear and cold, but there had been some light rain. They marched fifteen hours. The rain began again in earnest that night once the men went into camp, two miles north of Henryville.[423]

NEARING COLUMBIA: SATURDAY, NOVEMBER 26, 1864

Saturday morning, November 26, broke rainy and very muddy.[424] Once again, the army was up and out and on the road at sunrise. Their quarry, Schofield's army, was now in Columbia, still hoping to get to Nashville.

Brigadier General John Adams's brother Thomas Patton Adams had received a promotion to major and was commissary of subsistence for his brother's brigade.[425] They and many others in Hood's army were moving ever closer to familiar territory. They marched through the little village of Mount Pleasant and on into Maury County. Adams's brigade and the rest of the Army of Tennessee went on half rations. There was plenty of parched corn to go around but not much else.[426] Rain continued as the army trudged on toward Columbia via the Mount Pleasant and Columbia Pike, but morale was good. They made camp that night eight miles south of Columbia.[427]

One of the soldiers in the Confederate ranks was a native of Maury County, Tennessee. His name was Samuel Rush Watkins, and many years after the war, he wrote a memoir entitled *Co. Aytch*. Watkins recalled how he and the other Tennesseans felt as they marched deeper into their home country: "How every pulse did beat and leap, and how every heart did throb with emotions of joy, which seemed nearly akin to heaven, when we received the glad intelligence of our onward march toward the land of promise, and of our loved ones."[428]

In another part of the Confederate advance, Major General Patrick Cleburne rode with his troops. He took note of a lovely church, St. John's Episcopal, that sat just to the right of the road. This was the church that Leonidas Polk and his brothers had built years before. Cleburne paused as his columns pushed north. Dismounting, he slowly walked around the grounds of that lovely church and remarked to one of his officers, "It is almost worth dying for, to be buried in such a beautiful spot."[429]

POISED TO ATTACK: SUNDAY, NOVEMBER 27, 1864

Sunday, November 27, broke warm and cloudy, but the recent rains made the marching difficult through the mud.[430] Intermittent showers plagued the advance. Adams's men broke camp and began their march to Columbia at sunrise. The Federals still occupied the town and had taken up a defensive position south of the Duck River. From a hill, Confederate scouts observed the enemy soldiers. The Confederates prepared to attack at daybreak.[431]

The Sun Appears: Monday, November 28, 1864

The Confederate army rushed into Columbia before dawn, but their quarry was gone. Famished Southern soldiers broke into stores and helped themselves to whatever they could find. The retreating Federals burned the railroad bridge over the Duck River and set up defensive positions on the north side to guard potential crossing points. Forrest's cavalry managed to ford the river, and Hood brought up his trusty pontoons and prepared to cross his army the next morning.[432]

That night, General Adams and other officers dined at the home of James H. Thomas in Columbia. Bishop Dr. Charles Todd Quintard would note in his diary that Adams was in "high glee" at the affair.[433]

The Incident at Spring Hill: Tuesday, November 29, 1864

After weeks of mostly rain and cold and snow, the day promised to be fair. The Federals were on the north side of the river, and the Southern army intended to flank them. To that end, Hood ordered his men to cross the Duck at Davis Ford, east of Columbia. By 9:00 a.m., Stewart's corps, with Adams's brigade, was across the river. Hood rode in advance with Cleburne's men. The sky was clear and bright, almost balmy. The downside to the warmth was the mud. A Confederate noted, "We sank at every step in mud over our shoes."[434] Before they marched from Alabama, Hood had promised that he would fight on ground of his choosing, and the men's spirits were high. Now they were closing in on their first target: Schofield. Once across the Duck River, Stewart's corps traveled north via Davis Ford Road to Spring Hill. This turned out to be a bad choice because the old, seldom-used back road was in bad shape and the marching men churned the ground into a quagmire, which tired out the soldiers.[435]

In their front, the Southerners could make out Federal troops along a ridge. Hood worried that the Federals would flank him. He halted the army for lunch at noon. A young boy along the road had some slaves roll out hogsheads of tobacco and offered it to the soldiers. A woman fried up two hogs for the passing troops.[436] Yes, despite the hard march along the bad road, this was a fine day, and things seemed to keep getting better.

By around 3:00 p.m., Stewart's corps approached Rutherford Creek, just southeast of Spring Hill. They heard shooting coming from the direction of the town where Forrest was battling with Federal infantry and waiting for his own infantry to come up in support. Stewart's corps was held in reserve on the south side of Rutherford Creek, two and a half miles south of the turnpike. Throughout the rest of the day, the Confederates seemed not to know exactly what to do. Cleburne's division, along with Bell's dismounted cavalry, fought the Northerners while most of the remainder of the Southern army waited around.[437] After several hours of waiting in the dark, Stewart's corps, including Adams's brigade, finally received orders and moved north to take a position just off the turnpike, about a mile north of Spring Hill. On their way to their assigned position, they were halted by a staff officer who claimed to have orders from Hood that indicated Stewart was to move his troops even farther away from the road. His corps bivouacked around ten or eleven o'clock that night while Stewart rode to Hood's headquarters and attempted to get clarification on these new orders.[438] Had they gotten to the road, they could have shut off the Federal route to Franklin, but they did not. Nor did any of the other Confederate troops who were so close to the road. As a result, none of the Confederates moved up to the turnpike. The tired men of the entire Army of Tennessee built campfires and ate their meager rations. Hood retired for the night at a nearby plantation, Oak Lawn.[439]

The field where A.P. Stewart's corps, including Adams's brigade, waited for orders on the evening of November 29, 1864. *Photo by John Lane.*

Sometime during the same night, John McAllister Schofield pulled off one of the oddest, most sensational moves of the entire war. Without lights or markers, he marched his entire army up the dark turnpike, past the sleeping Confederate army (who were, in some cases, camped just a few hundred yards off the road) and on to Franklin. He just followed the road and hoped he would not be stopped. He was not. How could thousands of Federal soldiers, hundreds of horses and mules, scores of loaded wagons and limbers and caissons of artillery move north along that turnpike and not be stopped? This would later and forever after be known as the "Incident at Spring Hill." There have been attempts to explain what happened that night. Hood blamed Cheatham. Stewart blamed Hood. Regardless of who was to blame, the fact remained that the Federal army had moved on to the protection of Franklin. When Hood found out the next morning that his grand scheme had been undone, he was furious.[440]

Chapter 32

"The Fate of a Soldier"

Franklin, Tennessee, Wednesday, November 30, 1864

Wednesday, November 30, broke cold and clear but with a promise of warmth. Many would later describe the day as "mild" and like "Indian summer." Indian summer is a brief, warm and hazy time that interrupts the cold of late fall or winter. Although it does not last long, it is glorious.

Hood began the day hosting a breakfast at a lovely local home named Rippavilla. There, he advised his generals what they already knew: the Federals had eluded them once again. The Kentuckian then put his troops on the road in pursuit of Schofield. As they marched, the bedraggled butternuts marveled at the waste of the fleeing Federals. The route was littered with packs and equipment, burning wagons and even mules, shot dead in their traces, all discarded by the Northerners in their race north to Franklin.[441] The Confederates were greeted as conquerors all along the march. Women cheered and gave them bread.[442] Boys rushed to the roadside, encouraging the soldiers, "Push on, boys, you will capture all the Yanks soon."[443] The warmth of the day, the evidence of a hurried escape by their foes and the joy that greeted them lifted the men's spirits.

The Army of Tennessee included men from all over the Confederate States of America. There were troops from Alabama, South Carolina, Mississippi, Georgia, Louisiana, Texas, North Carolina, Missouri, Tennessee, Florida, Kentucky and Arkansas.[444] The Tennesseans were fighting to drive the invaders from their native soil. All of the men moved forward, encouraged by what they were seeing and hearing on this advance.

The road rose slightly and then flattened out going through Spring Hill but rose to crest a hill just before Thompson's Station. There had been a battle here the year before, and Forrest's beloved horse, Roderick, died in a charge and was buried east of the road. To the left or west as they marched were gentle, rolling hills, typical of this area. To the right, in the distance, were more hills. North of Thompson's Station, the road undulated. They crossed the West Harpeth River, and the road curved to the left as they began the final approach to Franklin.

Adams eased Old Charley north, watching over his men as they marched on the familiar road. His division commander, William Wing Loring, known as "Old Blizzards" because of his rallying cry in battle, "Give 'em blizzards, boys!" rode with the troops.[445] Lieutenant Colonel Rorer wrote, "They call him this because he always wants the artillery men to give the yankees a Blizzard when they come in the way. I do not know whether he means by that case shot, Canister, or What and I do not think the artillerist know, but they always shoot some thing.…It almost seems he can curse a cannon up hill without horses. His anger is terrible and his power of vituperative language almost inconceivable."[446] Adams's corps commander, Alexander Peter Stewart, also rode with the troops. Nicknamed "Old Straight" for his "devotion to clarity and precision," Stewart was a native of Tennessee and, after graduating from West Point, ended up teaching mathematics and natural history at Cumberland University in Lebanon. Now, Stewart was moving forward, toward Franklin, with his men.[447]

Stewart's corps led the march to Franklin. Around noon, riders from Forrest's cavalry approached to warn them that the Federal rearguard had formed a line across the pike, just ahead, along the southern slopes of Winstead Hill and Breezy Hill. Hood ordered Stewart to peel off to the right and flank the Federal troops out of their position.[448] At Henpeck Lane, Stewart's corps turned east and followed that road to the Lewisburg Pike. This would be the last time John Adams would ever see his familiar road. The flanked Federals pulled back, and Stewart's corps gathered near John McGavock's home, known as Carnton, and awaited orders while the rest of the army continued north.[449] The men stretched out on the cool grass and enjoyed the day as best they could.

Meanwhile, John Bell Hood, as his army hurried northward, rode ahead and hobbled up Winstead Hill to look across the field and consider his options. Scanning the distant Federal works south of Franklin, he saw

General Hood's view from Winstead Hill, taken after the war. In the bottom image, the Franklin-Columbia Turnpike is the white strip angling to the right. *Library of Congress*. The top image shows the same view today. *Photo by John Lane*.

the enemy waiting for him. The blue lines were centered on the road and the Carter House. All Schofield really wanted to do was cross the Harpeth River and move on to Nashville, but he had to stop in Franklin in order to get his wagon trains across the Harpeth. Hood would not allow this. The Kentuckian turned to a fellow officer and exclaimed, "We will make the fight!"[450] Hood convened a council of war at the house of William Harrison, just south of Winstead Hill. As he laid out his plans, his generals could not believe what they were hearing, and some voiced their concerns. Despite the protestations of his subordinates, Hood ordered a frontal assault, with very little artillery support and certainly no preparatory bombardment.[451]

The men of Adams's brigade were not privy to the meeting. What they knew was what they could see and feel and hear. And what they saw before them was a beautiful valley. They knew that beyond the distant hills was Nashville. They also saw men in blue uniforms busily fortifying every inch of ground south of town, where these Confederates would have to pass. They watched the Northerners move cannons into place. Bayonets gleamed in the fading light of this late autumn day. It was almost 3:00 p.m.

On the Confederate right, the eastern flank, where Loring's division would advance, the Harpeth River angles in toward Franklin. Because they could not go around, over or through this natural barrier, soldiers advancing here would be funneled into a killing zone. The fields were open and flat. Near the Federal lines, there was a railroad. Federal breastworks began on the other side of the tracks. There were also heavy Osage orange hedges along the Lewisburg Pike and in front of the Federal works.[452]

Osage oranges, or "hedge apples," are large, green, lumpy fruit often found on the ground in autumn. The French called the tree *bois d'arc* or bow wood because Native Americans used the prized branch wood to produce exceptional bows. American settlers found other uses for this tree. One use was as a hedge. When Osage orange trees were planted closely together in a line, they were an early version of barbed wire because not only were the branches tough to deal with, but there were also long, sharp thorns that could tear through flesh. A good Osage orange hedge was "horse high, bull strong, and hog tight," meaning high enough that a horse could not jump over it, strong enough that a bull couldn't fight his way through and tight enough that a hog could not make its way through the hedge.[453]

As if the hedges were not formidable enough, the Federal troops bolstered their already strong defensive position by cutting off the tops of the hedge, interlocking them and placing them directly in front of, and approximately thirty feet from, their lines. The Federals added sharpened planks, secured

Osage orange hedge thorns. This photo was taken on November 28, 2016, so this is how the hedges were when the Federals fashioned their fiendish barrier. *Photo by Professor Alan Windham, University of Tennessee Ag Extension.*

in the ground and angled so as to hit an approaching enemy in the chest. Fifty to one hundred yards from the railroad were two batteries of artillery, one with four guns, one with six. They were situated on a hill and had a fine field of fire.[454] Inside the works, near Mr. Carter's cotton gin, were two more guns. Across the Harpeth River, Fort Granger would fire its three-inch ordnance rifled guns unopposed into the ranks of the Southerners.[455]

The Federal left would confront the Confederate right. There were three brigades there, behind breastworks. Israel Stiles commanded the 120th, 63rd and 128th Indiana and the 112th Illinois. John Steven "Jack" Casement would lead the 65th Illinois, 65th Indiana, 124th Indiana and 5th Tennessee. And James Reilly led the 100th and 104th Ohio. These midwesterners would oppose Stewart's corps. The total of these three Federal brigades was around five thousand men. Besides Stewart's corps, the dismounted cavalry of Abraham Buford and Cleburne's troops of Cheatham's division would advance against this position.[456]

The Sixty-Fifth Illinois fought at Franklin under Lieutenant Colonel William Scott Stewart. Some of the Sixty-Fifth Illinois and a company of the Sixty-Fifth Indiana were armed with breech-loading, repeating rifles.[457] Company A of the Sixty-Fifth Indiana was armed with sixteen-shot, .44-caliber, Henry repeating rifles.[458] The Henry was a technological marvel. During the course of the war, some 10,000 Henry rifles were produced. Only 1,700 were officially purchased; the rest were bought by individuals. At a cost of forty dollars each, they were not cheap, but they were deadly. Henry agent Jonathan W. Brown of Columbus, Ohio, touted the rifle, "Penetration at 100 yards is 8″ At 400 yards 5″ and it carries with force sufficient to kill at 1,000 yards." After one battle, a captured Confederate said, "Your rapid firing confused our men; they thought the devil helped you, and it was no use to fight."[459]

In the Southern lines, this was a time of final things: final thoughts, final goodbyes, final looks around at the beauty of a late autumn day and, in at least one case, a final feast. Captain J.T. Smith of Company E, Fifteenth Mississippi, had relatives nearby. As the troops milled about, waiting, Smith took a "French leave" and snuck away for a few hours to meet with his kin. Ever mindful of his comrades in arms, he returned with rations for his buddies, Lieutenants T.H. Allen and C.H. Campbell. They invited their commander, Michael Farrell. Lieutenant Colonel Walter A. Rorer and Major William F. Crumpton also received and accepted an invitation to this last supper.[460]

As they ate, they talked about home and familiar dead. Their thoughts turned at last to their chances of making it to tomorrow. Captain Smith looked sad and said, "Well, we are going to have a hard fight, and it will be my last. I think I will be killed." Allen said, "I am ready to go. If my country requires my life, I am willing to yield it." Rorer said, "If things continue as they now are, it will only be a question of time when every true Confederate who stands at his post must be killed, as we have no place to get recruits and are fighting ten to one at present. It is a mere question of time when we must all go, and I came out for that purpose." Crumpton agreed. Farrell said, "O, well boys, that is a soldier's life. Let us not complain or shrink from it." (In a letter written to his cousin earlier in the year, Rorer may have summed up this fatalistic feeling best when he wrote, "To many the bitterness of death is past long before death intervenes to stop their mortal cares. It is astonishing how little men who are constantly exposed and who have to endure much suffering fear death. There are doubtless many men in this war who would welcome death as a relief from all their troubles and sufferings.") Before the night was out, all of them would be dead or mortally wounded except Campbell.[461]

There could be little doubt Hood intended to fight. He had marched the remainder of his army up through the opening between Winstead Hill and Breezy Hill. They filed into place in plain view of the enemy. To the left of Adams's position, the Army of Tennessee stretched as far as the eye could see. Nearly twenty thousand hungry, tired, dirty, anxious men and boys

The front of John McGavock's home, Carnton. Adams's brigade waited nearby before the battle. *Photo by Randy Duncan.*

waited for a command that would send this army of ghosts into the sunset. Behind them were the losses at Fort Donelson, Perryville, Shiloh, Vicksburg, Chattanooga and Atlanta. Around them were the still-living great names of the Confederate West: Cleburne, Forrest, Stewart, Cheatham and Hood. You did not have to be a veteran or a West Point graduate to understand what would happen once the Rebels moved forward. A teenage soldier in the Southern ranks looked across the field, sized up the situation, turned to his friend and said, "This don't look too good."[462]

Perhaps sensing the apprehension among their ranks, a Southern band struck up "Dixie." If this tune still stirs emotions in listeners 150 years later, imagine what it must have meant to those men that day. "Dixie" was part anthem, part hymn, part battle cry, and when the men in the tattered gray lines heard its familiar strains, they raised from their souls 4 years of deprivation and loss and fury and let forth the famed Rebel yell. The shrill, high-pitched tremolo echoed off the hillsides and rang back on the Southerners. Across the valley, some two miles distant, a Federal band responded with "Hail Columbia." The Northerners shouted their throaty reply.[463]

Stewart's corps would advance on the Federal works with Winfield Scott Featherston's and Thomas Moore Scott's brigades in advance and Adams

The Carter House witnessed intense fighting the night of November 30. *Photo by Randy Duncan.*

This building on the property of the Carter House in Franklin, Tennessee, still bears the scars of battle. Note the bullet holes. *Photo by Randy Duncan.*

in reserve. When they stepped off, John Adams's brigade was to keep about one hundred yards in the rear. Featherston would move ahead on the left and Scott on the right. They would march past Carnton and on to Franklin. Federal soldiers sat on top of their works, staring at the almost unbelievable sight. There, in front of them, was an entire Confederate army, stretched from one end of the field to the other. Couriers and officers on horseback galloped back and forth. Flags flapped and fluttered in the cool breeze. Bands played. There was no wilderness or cornfield or mountain to block the view. It was a magnificent scene, and one they would never forget.[464] One Federal soldier recalled, "It was worth a year of one's lifetime to witness the marshalling and advance of the rebel lines of battle."[465]

During the war, Albert Sidney Johnston had ridden his horse, Fire Eater, into battle. Robert E. Lee rode his horse, Traveler, to victory. And Nathan Bedford Forrest terrorized Federal soldiers astride his steeds Roderick and, later, King Phillip. Now, as he had done many times before, John Adams hooked his foot into the stirrup and pulled himself up onto his beloved warhorse, Old Charley. Thomas Gibson noted that Adams was "calm and self-possessed, vigilantly watching and directing the movements of his men."[466] Gibson described his cousin as "a superb horseman, and picturesque when mounted."[467]

Around four o'clock, an order was given, and without the benefit of a preparatory bombardment, the gray lines lurched forward toward Franklin. These men were veterans of many battles. There could have been no question about what awaited them. But they moved forward anyway. They proudly unfurled and displayed their tattered battle flags. The Southern bands played "Dixie," "Bonnie Blue Flag," "Ben Bolt" and "The Girl I Left Behind Me." Confederate Dr. Phillips of the Twenty-Second Mississippi recalled, "This was the first and only time I ever heard our bands playing upon a battlefield at the beginning of a charge."[468]

Although there were no "Bonnie Blue" flags carried onto the field that day, the last verse of the song of that name perhaps summed up this scene best:

Then here's to our Confederacy,
Strong are we and brave;
Like patriots of old we'll fight
Our heritage to save.
And rather than submit to shame,
To die we would prefer;

So cheer for the Bonnie Blue Flag
That bears a single star.

The Federal men, despite the marvelous and awesome display before them, could not let themselves be swayed by sentimentality. These were tough men and veterans of many battles as well. There was a job to do, and they would do it. They would stand and fight and hold their positions. On the far left of the Federal lines, the soldiers waited for the Confederates to come into range. Jack Casement had an idea to get his men's attention and focus their efforts.

Before (and after) the war, Casement was a railroad man. He was tough as nails and used to leading rough men in hard situations.[469] As the Rebels advanced, Casement, all five feet four inches of him, jumped on top of the rampart and yelled to his soldiers, "Men, do you see those damned Rebel sons of bitches coming?" They replied with a yell. "Well, I want you to stand here like rocks and whip hell out of them." Then he emptied his revolver in the direction of the approaching Southerners.[470]

Around 4:10 p.m., the Confederates were still one thousand yards from the Federal works when Fort Granger's guns opened fire. The first shell fell short. The advance continued. The second shell flew long. The third shell burst among the Thirty-Fifth Alabama. Body parts flew. There were shrieks of pain. Dead men lay on the field, the first fruits of Franklin.[471] The gray tide rolled forward. The Southerners moved forward, marching steadily over the soft fields. At about eight hundred yards, Federal artillery from the lines in front opened up. Shells burst and fragments hissed through the air. General Adams steadied his men and urged Charley toward the distant Federal works. Men were falling, screaming, dying. Around four hundred yards out, the Federals opened up with rifle fire and canister. "Canister" was small iron balls packed into metal cans. These cans were loaded into the cannon like any other projectile; however, when the gun was fired, the can burst and the metal balls shot through the air, turning a cannon into a very large, longer-range shotgun. The metal balls smashed bones, shredded skin and tore through the ranks, leaving great gaps where once there were marching men. Mangled bodies dropped to the bloodying ground. Pitiful cries for help came up from friends, and still the Southerners marched toward the enemy. Bullets, canister balls and other shells shrieked and smashed all around them. There was no respite from the storm of lead and iron.[472] Some of the Southern soldiers literally pulled their hats over their faces in the face of the fire, as if to protect themselves from a hail storm.[473]

Even advancing in the rear, shot and shell passed over and through the front lines and into Adams's men. The General kept his brigade moving forward, and then, out of the chaos and din, a single Federal bullet tore into Adams's right shoulder. He reeled in his saddle and clutched at the severe wound. Blood stained his uniform. His staff officers rushed over and begged him to leave the field and seek immediate treatment. John Adams could have left right then, received treatment for his wound and likely survived the battle and possibly the war. Georgie and the children were anxiously waiting for word that he would be coming home as he had always managed to do in the past. No one would have questioned his bravery or commitment to "the cause." But he did not leave. Whatever he had done or not done up to this point in his military career, he would forever after be known for what he now decided. He shouted to his staff, "No; I am going to see my men through."[474]

The Harpeth River forced Stewart's corps toward the center, bunching the Southern troops into a densely packed target. A member of Scott's brigade, Joseph Nicholas Thompson of the Thirty-Fifth Alabama, remembered, "General Adams…who had the reserve, rode so close to me that I thought he would slip on me."[475] As they approached the Federal works, the road rose slightly, forming a slight ridge near the Collins farm, south of the railroad tracks and the murderous fire just beyond. It was 4:25 p.m., and the sun continued sinking below the horizon.[476]

Featherston's advance was stopped in the railroad cut and to the west of the Lewisburg Pike. Scott's badly battered men began falling back. Adams, still bleeding from his wound, rode Old Charley back and forth, leading on his men and looking for a way forward. He moved his brigade behind the rise along the southern side of the Nashville and Decatur Railroad tracks in an attempt to shield them from the Federal fire. Captain John L. Collins of the Fifteenth Mississippi was at the General's side. Adams turned to Collins and ordered him to take the Fifteenth to the right to ease off the overlapping. Collins, astride a loudly braying mule, rode untouched through the mêlée and found Colonel Farrell leading the Fifteenth forward. Collins could distinctly hear Farrell calming his men: "Steady, men, steady, men." Collins rode over and delivered Adams's order to Farrell, who replied, "John, I am doing the best I can, you see."[477]

Despite all the deadly fire poured into them, the gray tide had swept across nearly two miles of open ground, but their advance broke at the Osage orange hedge. The Southern troops advancing up the Columbia Pike, near the center of the advance, actually managed to penetrate the Federal lines at one point until being driven back by a determined counterattack, but

A modern-day view from the Collins Farm. Lewisburg Pike is on the right, and the railroad tracks can be seen in the distance. *Photo by Randy Duncan.*

here, on the Confederate right, the eastern flank, this hedge was stopping the men in gray. Looking for an opening so his troops could move forward, Adams rode left. He directed his cousin Thomas Gibson to the right and Patrick Henry to the left. Adams informed them, "I can be found in the center if needed."[478] The Federals continued firing into the bunched mass of men. One of Adams's soldiers, Private Wesley P. Peacock of the Fifteenth Mississippi, had gone into the battle armed only with an axe. He put it to use now chopping away at the barrier.[479] Finally, there was an opening in the hedge. Seeing this, Adams and Old Charley pushed through. A Mississippian grabbed the colors, followed Adams and shouted to his fellow soldiers, "Come this way, boys!"[480] Adams turned and shouted, "Men, follow me!"[481] James Binford later wrote, "History has never done him justice, and I hope Tennesseans will see to it that the page that records his deeds is one of the brightest that adorns Southern History, for she never gave the South a truer, braver, officer."[482]

In later years, a Federal soldier who was fighting against Adams's advance that night wrote to one of his former foes, "Your men went down like leaves in the Fall of the year." He went on to describe what he had seen and how he marveled at the courage of his enemy. But, he noted, "the one great spirit who appealed the strongest to our admiration was General John Adams. He rode along his line and became conspicuous while he was quite a little distance out, We could plainly see he was very intent on something, and he was the one of all the others that we were to do business with. As he came closer and closer he seemed to be more and more intent. He was riding forward through such a rain of bullets that no one had any reason to believe that he would escape them all, but he seemed to be in the hands of the Unseen."[483]

At 4:45 p.m., Adams spurred Old Charley forward. The warhorse, a bay, had come all the way from California with Adams and his family and still had the "U.S." brand on his left hip and, according to one chronicler, "was almost as well known in the army as his master." Thomas Gibson noted that Old Charley "had that peculiar habit, noticed in a number of prominent officers' horses during the war, of sometimes squatting close to the ground when under fire. I was adjutant general on General Adams' staff, and have seen the horse do this many times."[484] Charley did not squat down now. He obeyed his master's command.

All the roads of John Adams's life led to this small stretch of earth and the Federal lines beyond. The General and his beloved horse had covered countless miles, and now they would ride into eternity together. Adams

Mr. Carter's cotton gin. Cotton taken from this building would be used as a pillow for John Adams at the last. *Courtesy of the Heritage Foundation of Franklin and Williamson County.*

leaned forward, and Old Charley pounded across the last few yards. Seeing this lone rider emerge from the hedge and the haze, Colonel Stewart, of the Sixty-Fifth Illinois, screamed to his men not to fire on the brave Confederate officer,[485] but Adams intended to take this line, and as Old Charley made his final leap onto the earthworks, John Adams reached for the colors of the Sixty-Fifth Illinois. As he grabbed at the flag, the color guard fired.[486] In an instant, their ride was over. Old Charley's lifeless form tumbled onto the top of the parapet. General Adams, badly wounded, toppled under his horse. His men continued to press forward into the storm of death but could not reach the Federal works.

At 5:05 p.m., in the west, the last light faded, and then darkness covered the valley.[487]

Adams's Mississippians bravely rushed the lines and died. Finally, they could no longer absorb the deadly fire, and they fell back into the night. In the course of the evening, there were as many as nine distinct charges made by these men, but they accomplished nothing, save for adding to the long list of dead and wounded.[488]

During a lull between attacks, Federal soldiers pulled the General from under Old Charley. The horse, faithful unto death, lay with his forelegs over the works. A later writer would claim that, in death, Charley's final aspect was "almost as striking as the lion of Thorwaldsen," the famed Lion of Lucerne.[489] The Federals moved Adams away from the fighting and laid

An artist's rendition of Adams's and Old Charley's final moments. *From* Battles and Sketches of the Army of Tennessee.

Noted Civil War historian Thomas Cartwright believes this ravine, behind the new park trail, is where the Federals placed Adams. *Photo by author.*

The saddle pulled from Old Charley's body by Federals. The bullet holes in it are reminders of the horrible last moments of the General and his beloved warhorse. *Courtesy of the Tennessee State Museum.*

him down on the cold ground. The General was conscious and groaned in pain. He asked if he could be returned to his men. He was told no, they could not do that, the battle was still raging. He asked for water. A Federal soldier cradled the General's head and put a canteen to his lips. Adams thanked his enemy for his kindness. Another midwesterner brought an armload of cotton from the gin to put beneath Adams's head as a pillow. The din of the battle receded from his ears and the light faded. The Federal soldiers told him how sorry they were for his sad fate. Adams's last words, as reported by a Federal officer who was there, were, "It is the fate of a soldier to die for his country."[490] And then, as Captain Collins of the Fifteenth Mississippi would remember, the General passed "to the reward of as noble a soldier as ever gave his life to his native land. Would that I might see him on his old horse Charley."[491]

Chapter 33

The Final Journey

The Confederate attacks failed that night, and the Federal lines remained intact. As he had intended all along, Schofield evacuated Franklin, withdrawing the last of his main force around 2:00 a.m. on December 1, having accomplished what he had set out to do all along, which was get his supply wagons across the river. Hood did not know Schofield had left Franklin and decided to attack again in the morning. He brought up his artillery this time. He explained, after the battle, that he had not used his artillery the day before, November 30, because he did not want to risk hurting women and children. His report read, "The artillery was instructed to take no part in the engagement, on account of the danger to which women and children in the village would be exposed."[492] He intended to use his artillery this morning, but there was no need. Once again, Schofield was gone. Around 4:00 a.m., Confederate infantry moved into the abandoned town.[493]

The long night ended. Dawn found the field strewn with dead and wounded. Even people who were there could never really comprehend the awful scene or describe it. Of this battle, Sam Watkins wrote:

> *Kind reader, right here my pen, and courage, and ability fail me....I was there. I saw it. My flesh trembles, and creeps, and crawls when I think of it today. My heart almost ceases to beat at the horrid recollection....I cannot describe it. It beggars description. I will not attempt to describe it. I could not. The death-angel was there to gather its last harvest.*[494]

The back porch of Carnton, where they laid Adams's body after the battle and where Gibson went to retrieve his beloved cousin's remains. *Photo by Randy Duncan.*

A cold, strong wind added to the misery. Indian summer was over as fast as it had begun. In places, the Confederate dead were stacked like cordwood where they had fallen in front of the Federal works. Search parties looked for the downed officers. Major General Patrick Cleburne was dead. Brigadier General Otto Strahl was dead. Brigadier General States Rights Gist was

Above: John Adams's military headstone in Maplewood Cemetery in Pulaski. *Photo by Randy Duncan.*

Left: The Adams-Woodward monument at the Maplewood Cemetery in Pulaski, Tennessee. General Adams's military headstone is directly behind this monument. *Photo by Randy Duncan.*

wounded and would soon be dead. Brigadier General Hiram Granbury was dead. Brigadier General John Carter was wounded and would die of his wounds ten days later. And John Adams was dead. In all, 6 Confederate generals died as a result of the Battle of Franklin. Officially, Hood reported his losses as more than 6,000 casualties including more than 1,700 killed.[495] Some later estimates put the figure closer to 7,300 casualties.[496] Adams's brigade suffered 44 killed, 271 wounded and 22 missing, for a total of 337.[497]

A Confederate burial detail found John Adams behind the Federal lines. Old Charley's lifeless body draped the parapet. The sad detail placed Adams's body into an ambulance next to Patrick Cleburne's lifeless form. They were taken to Carnton Plantation, and their bodies were laid on the back porch.[498] Just twenty-four hours before, the Army of Tennessee had moved forward, encouraged and emboldened. Now the army gathered its brave dead and tended its wounded. The army itself would never recover from that long, terrible night.

Thomas Gibson, himself painfully wounded during the battle, went to Carnton and received permission to take his cousin's body. The General was prepared for burial and placed in a cedar casket, procured in Franklin by order of General Hood. Gibson knew where to take the body of his cousin. For all the miles he had traveled, all the places he had lived and seen, General Adams had always claimed Pulaski and Tennessee as home.

Now the General had one final journey to make. Using army transportation, Thomas Gibson and General Adams's body servant, Billie, began the two-day-long trek back down the familiar road, carrying the General home to rest forever by his mother and father, beneath the trees of Pulaski.[499]

Chapter 34

"Where No Sorrows Come"

When word reached Georgiana of her husband's death, she fought through her grief and moved with her six children from Alabama to stay at the home of her sister-in-law Anne Adams in Pulaski, Tennessee. Just a few years before, John Adams and two of his brothers had lovingly and thoughtfully cared for Anne after the death of their mother. Now Anne would help her brother's widow and children in their time of need. The war continued to rage on, but it was drawing to a close when a letter arrived from Georgiana's father, Charles McDougall:

Philadelphia, Pa. Feb. 14th, '65
To Miss A. (Anne) Adams
My dear Friend:

We are a thousand times obliged for your last favor. The sad detail of my dear son's fate with its sorrows had much of comfort. Long before I dreamed of any nearer situation between John and myself we were mess mates on an Indian campaign, and on which begun our friendship.

Our relation of father and son were those of very tender and strong attachment—in him was all a father could wish—We loved him as we did our own children who all loved him as their own brother, and in all our intercourse as with every member of my family, not a word or look or thought to mar our happiness.

He loved Georgie as he did his life, even more, and not a wish had she but it was always anticipated. At one time Georgie was suddenly very ill. I despaired of her life and I thought it advisable to tell him. When I did so he fell as if shot in overpowering grief—and when the crisis was past and announced, his joy knew no bounds—the happiest man I ever saw.

He was fun, without guile, chivalrous, affectionate and all that relatives or friends could wish him. He leaves in his example a rich legacy to his children—God bless them.

How much we have desired to see you all and mix our griefs and tears with yours, to unburden our hearts as cannot be done by writing. Tell my darling daughter that she and her dear ones are never out of our thoughts—that although she has kind and loving friends, who will do everything for her, yet her father's home is where she ought and must come to. What little of life which is left to her parents will be devoted to her and the children, and we pray our Heavenly Father that we may live for their sakes.

Please mention to Georgie to notify me that she will come and when, so that I can prepare. Her mother and myself will meet her wherever she may indicate. Early information will govern the time I shall rent her a house which now are hard to procure.

And now dear Sister of my beloved son (now in Heaven) accept from us our deep and sincere condolence and we pray God to sustain you in your affliction and that we may all meet where no sorrows come.

C. McDougall[500]

Chapter 35

Tennessee Hero

Helen Plane believed in remembering. She remembered, for instance, that she and her husband, William, met at a party while playing a game of Blind Man's Bluff.[501] They married soon afterward and began their life together. When the Civil War broke out, William joined the Confederate army and led the "Baker County Fire-Eaters" until his death at Antietam in 1862.[502] Mrs. Plane never forgot him or his service. She went on to become the president of the Atlanta Chapter of the United Daughters of the Confederacy. In that role, she addressed a large crowd on November 9, 1895, that had come to dedicate relics of the late war.

The program opened with a band playing "Maryland, My Maryland." Mrs. Plane then rose to speak. She welcomed the visitors to Atlanta and spoke reverently of those who had given their lives for the Lost Cause. Near the end of her speech, she reminded the listeners, "We are in part the sentinels guarding the bivouac of the dead. We are the true chroniclers of their valor. Our deeds and their precious memories must be kept perennial in the hearts of our children."[503]

In 1909, then eighty-year-old Mrs. Plane championed a plan for sculptors to carve the likenesses of the great heroes of the South, Robert E. Lee, Thomas "Stonewall" Jackson and Jefferson Davis, into the side of Stone Mountain, Georgia. Planners of the project asked each state of the former Confederacy to nominate its greatest heroes to immortalize in smaller carvings at Stone Mountain. Among the names selected were J.E.B. Stuart, Joseph E. Johnston and A.P. Hill from Virginia; Patrick Cleburne of Arkansas; P.G.T. Beauregard of Louisiana; and Earl Van Dorn of Mississippi.

During the Civil War, the state of Tennessee sent more than 100,000 men to fight for the Southern cause.[504] Of those, the Volunteer State selected as its heroes the "Wizard of the Saddle," Nathan Bedford Forrest; Felix Zollicoffer, one of the first Confederate generals killed in the war;[505] William Brimage Bate, who ended the war a major general;[506] Benjamin Franklin "Frank" Cheatham, who helped raise the Provisional Army of Tennessee and ended the war a lieutenant general;[507] the famed "boy hero" Sam Davis; and Brigadier General John Adams.[508]

Chapter 36

A Day to Remember

November 30, 1899

The dawn of the twentieth century was a month away. New technology and inventions would forever change the world. But the people gathering in Franklin, Tennessee, on November 30, 1899, did not come to look forward. No, this was a day to look back, a day to remember.

They began arriving early in the morning. They came by train, carriage, horseback and on foot. Hundreds of Confederate flags and thousands of yards of red and white bunting adorned houses and businesses. A band played at the depot as people made their way to this small town. A few minutes after ten o'clock, a lonesome-sounding whistle announced the arrival of the train from Nashville. Many in the crowd hurried to the depot to watch as the passengers arrived. Out stepped the honored guests and dignitaries. Then the veterans, dressed in their familiar, old, gray uniforms, walked into the sunlight. Some of the old soldiers chose to wear civilian clothes.

There were pretty girls in pretty dresses and handsome men on handsome horses. There were politicians and soldiers, men and women of all ages, all here, all waiting for the start of the great parade. In all, as many as ten thousand people descended on Franklin, Tennessee, for the thirty-fifth anniversary of the battle and the unveiling of a new monument, dedicated to the memory of Confederate soldiers. The statue of a lone Confederate would stand guard over the town.

The members of the anxious crowd moved back toward town and found vantage points along the streets. The participants took their places for the march. A warning tap of a drum sounded, and the lines lurched forward. The band played and officers led the way, followed by an open carriage carrying two little girls who would unveil the statue. Then, in columns of four, the veterans marched into the town that so many of their comrades died trying to take. The weather could not have been better, and the throngs were thrilled by the sights and sounds. As each group passed, the crowds cheered. Then came a white-draped float, pulled along by four horses, carrying nineteen beautiful young ladies from Williamson County, dressed in white robes with crimson sashes emblazoned in gold letters with the names of states and cities of the former Confederacy. Each young lady waved a Confederate flag. The crowd roared their approval. At last, the procession ended and the speeches and songs began. And then, by four o'clock, it was all over and the tired thousands made their way home.

In the crowd that day were many people who had a direct tie to that terrible evening thirty-five years before. There were men who would never, could never, describe the horrors of that night. There were widows and daughters and sons of Confederate veterans. But there was a particular guest who received "quite an ovation from the old boys in gray" and the citizens who had gathered when her presence was announced. She had come from St. Louis with the Missouri contingent and stood beside Dr. J.P. Hanner as he delivered his address of welcome to the crowd. That guest was General Adams's wife, Georgiana.[509]

November 30, 2014

It is the 150th anniversary of the battle.

We are at Winstead Hill. The speakers are concluding their talks. We started the day in Spring Hill, beside the field where Stewart's corps waited for the orders that came too late. Then we drove up U.S. 31 and turned right on Henpeck Lane and followed it until it dead-ends at the Lewisburg Pike. There we turned left, toward Franklin, following the route General Adams took. We stopped at Carnton and paused at the back porch. We left there and went to the Collins Farm, where we met a young man from Illinois who told us he had driven down that morning just because he felt like he needed to be here today.

The Collins Farm. *Photo by Randy Duncan.*

Now we look around and see all the people who have come to this hill, this night, to make this walk. There are reenactors and men in suits and people in shorts and jackets. There is talking, but it is quiet and somber.

Long shadows stretch into the valley. The sky is a blue-gray, and the fading sunlight shines through the low clouds.

Someone we do not see gives a signal, and the reenactors begin to form in rows of four and line up near the road. The next group in line is the flag-bearers. We fall in line behind them.

It is 4:00 p.m.

We begin the march to the Carter House. This busy road is congested, but tonight the traffic is stopped as we make our way north. All along the route, people are standing still, watching quietly. No one says a word. Some hold their hands over their hearts. Some take pictures. An elderly man is crying. This is not a celebration; it is a commemoration.

We crest a slight ridge and see that we still have a long way to go. Thirty minutes into the walk, we notice the air has cooled as the sun begins to disappear behind the hills. On this evening 150 years ago soldiers were dying, right here. The General was to our right with his men moving forward, toward Franklin, toward eternity.

It is 4:45 p.m.

Near the Carter House the light is nearly gone save for the glow from the thousands of luminaries flickering in the gathering darkness.

The march from Winstead Hill on the 150th anniversary of the Battle of Franklin, November 30, 2014. *Photo by Randy Duncan.*

Luminaries…Merriam-Webster defines a luminary as "1. A person of prominence or brilliant achievement 2. A body that gives light: one of the celestial bodies." Each luminary represents a man killed or wounded that night. There are more luminaries than you can count, lining the street, stretching as far as you can see. So many lights, so many lives that went out forever, here, 150 years ago.

There are families with little children. There are couples and people standing by themselves. You catch glimpses of their faces in the candlelight, here and gone, like a memory of someone you have lost.

It is 5:05 p.m.

In the west, the last light fades and darkness covers the valley. The march is over. In front of the Carter House, people find old friends and make new ones. We make our way back to our car, and on the way home, none of us says a word.

This was a day to remember.

Appendix A

Georgie and the Children

Charles McDougall Adams, born at Fort Craig, New Mexico, on April 5, 1855, and died in La Jolla, California, in June 1939.[510] Only nine when his father died, Charles went on to receive his education at St. Louis University and worked for railroads throughout his life, starting out as a clerk with the Iron Mountain Railway and ending up as a general agent for the El Paso and Southwestern Railway. He and his wife, Ellen "Nellie" Shobe Reaume Adams, had no children. He enjoyed hunting and fishing.[511]

Thomas Patton Adams, born in Baltimore on November 19, 1856, and died in 1920 in St. Louis. Patton had just turned eight when his father died. Like older brother Charles, he was also a railroad employee and worked as an agent for the Missouri–Iron Mountain Railways.[512] Patton and his wife, Katherine Duross, had two children, Georgiana McDougall Adams and Jane Duross Adams.[513]

John Adams, born in Washington, D.C., on May 15, 1858, and died of a heart attack on October 16, 1905, in St. Louis, Missouri. John was six when his father died at Franklin. Like his brothers before him, he worked for the railroad and was the chief of the department of claims and losses of the Wabash Railroad. In fact, when he died, his brothers Francis, Thomas Patton and Charles were all together in St. Louis tending to their sick mother.[514] He and his wife, Ida Belle Kinsella, had six children: Grace Marie, John, Oliver Buel Prince David, Lawrence Babbitt, Frances Joseph and Charles Thomas Dickson Adams.[515]

FRANCIS JOSEPH ADAMS, born in Fort Crook, California, on December 16, 1859. He learned of his father's death just before turning five. He graduated from Georgetown University in Washington, D.C., and became a doctor. Like his grandfather, he served as a doctor in the U.S. Army and participated in several expeditions in the West, as well as in the Philippines during the Spanish-American War.[516] He married Alice Conrad. They had one daughter, Mary Margaret Adams, who died in infancy.[517] His mother, Georgiana, came to live with them in Montana for a couple of years around the turn of the century. Dr. Adams died in an automobile accident in Montana in 1920.[518]

GEORGIANA MCDOUGALL ADAMS, born on December 16, 1861, in Memphis, Tennessee. She likely had no memories of her father, as she was just shy of three when her father died. She died on March 8, 1936, in Rochelle Park, New Jersey, at the home of her son Conde de Sales Pallen. She married Conde Benoist Pallen, a famous Catholic poet and essayist. Pallen's book *The Meaning of the Idylls of the King*, an interpretation of Alfred Lord Tennyson's work, drew this response from Tennyson himself: "You have seen further into the real meaning of the 'Idylls of the King' than any of my commentators." Their children were Charles McDougall, Conde de Sales, Esther Janet, Georgiana McDougall, Anne Elizabeth, Louise Auguste Benoist, Emma Mary, Frances Josephine, Louis Augusta, Thomas Adams and Montrose Benoist Pallen.[519]

EMMA PORTIS ADAMS, born on October 12, 1863, in Cahaba, Alabama. She died in 1946 and was buried in St. Louis, Missouri. She married John Murdoch Dickson in St. Louis. He was a lawyer in the city. They had no children.[520]

MRS. GEORGIANA MCDOUGALL ADAMS accepted her parents' invitation and moved in with them. Only twenty-nine when her husband died at Franklin, Georgiana raised their six children. She was a true widow of the South. When she attended the wedding of daughter Emma in St. Louis, in 1888, a newspaper article described Georgiana's dress: "Mrs. Adams wore a handsome mourning gown of black gros grain, heavily trimmed with crepe, the corsage made entirely of crepe, with crape lisse ruching at the throat and wrists."[521]

In May 1890, she attended another wedding, this one in Pulaski, Tennessee. Her niece Martha Adams was getting married. Martha had attended Emma's wedding, and now it was time to return the honor. This was Georgie's first trip back to Pulaski since the war. The newspaper noted, "She is well remembered here as the widow of Giles County's gallant son, Gen. John Adams, C.S.A. who laid down his life for the South in that wild rush that so nearly carried our 'Bonnie Blue Flag' over the Federal breast works at Franklin."[522]

The end for her came on a cold, late autumn night. Three of her children were born in December, and she passed away on Saturday, December 9, 1905, at 5:30 p.m., at her home on Maryland Avenue. She was seventy. Releases regarding her death were sent to Washington, D.C.; Indianapolis, Indiana; Great Falls, Montana; and Nashville, Tennessee.[523] On Tuesday, December 12, 1905, Georgiana McDougall Adams was laid to rest in Calvary Cemetery in St. Louis, Missouri, in a private ceremony. At last, she was free to join him.

He was waiting for her.

Appendix B

Where Did Adams Fall?

There is some question about where Adams fell during the battle. Despite the letters from Baker and Casement (below) and testimony of others who were at Franklin, some, including Federal generals John Casement and Jacob Cox, also said Adams fell outside the works. There is no way, now, to know for sure. Here are statements related to where Adams fell.

Bishop Charles Todd Quintard, writing in his diary on December 4, 1864, noted:

> *After breakfast I rode to Franklin to see Dr. Buist who is post surgeon. All along the way I found marks of the fight—dead horses, burnt wagons, etc., but at the line of breastworks at Mr. Carter's house where the heaviest fighting was done there was a great number of horses among which was poor John's white horse—within ten feet of the works. The horse of General Adams was further to the right just on top of the breastworks. Here the General had fallen, pierced by thirty or forty bullets.*[524]

Bishop Quintard's account is contemporary to the event (four days after), written in a diary in Franklin by a reliable source. This was not thirty years after the events, when memories could have been confused; this was less than a week after the battle, while the war was still raging. He was not trying to justify the Lost Cause; he was merely reporting what was then known or at least believed to be true.

The *Daily Constitutionalist* of Augusta, Georgia, on Thursday, March 16, 1865, wrote:

> *Sundry officers, says the* Montgomery Advertiser, *connected with the Military Department of Mississippi and the Post of Meridian, recently sent to the wife of Brig. Gen. John Adams, who was killed on the enemy's breastworks at Franklin, Tenn., $343 and other enclosures of importance, as a testimonial of the valuable services and sacrifices rendered the country by that gallant officer.*

Thomas Gibson, the General's cousin, who was at Franklin, recalled, "Gen. Adams death while in the act of leaping his horse (Old Charley) over the Federal breastworks, was one of the most heroic acts ever performed in any war that history records."[525]

Edward Adams Baker, a Federal officer, wrote, "The horse fell dead upon the top of the embankment and the General was caught under him, pierced with bullets."[526]

John Casement (Federal officer) wrote to Mrs. Adams, "It was my fortune to stand in our line within a foot of where the General succeeded in getting his horse's forelegs over the line." And later in the same letter, "Gen. Adams fell from his horse from the position in which the horse died, just over the line of works. Which were part breastworks and part ditch."[527] However, over the years, Casement also claimed that Adams had been killed outside the works, although he later changed that version to say that Adams had fallen outside the works where Casement's men found him still alive.[528]

Tom M. Gore of the Fifteenth Mississippi wrote that Old Charley died on the works and "Gen. Adams was wounded and retreated some thirty or forty paces from the works before he fell pierced with nine balls."[529]

O.W. Case of the Sixty-Fifth Illinois wrote that Adams died "150–200 yards from the works."[530]

James Barr, also of the Sixty-Fifth Illinois, wrote, "Our Colonel Casement (65th Illinois) tried hard to save the life of Gen. Adams of Mississippi. Col. Stewart called to our men not to fire on him, but it was too late. Adams rode his horse over the ditch to the top of the parapet, undertook to grasp the 'old flag' from the hands of our color sergeant, when he fell, horse and all, shot by the color guard."[531]

Tillman H. Stevens of Casement's brigade wrote, "Gen. Adams reached our line, but was shot down with his faithful horse, both falling together on top of the slight entrenchment that we had on this line."[532]

Major General Jacob Cox, a Federal officer, in his after-action report, written right after the battle, said, "One general officer (Adams) was shot down upon the parapet itself, his horse falling dead across the breastwork."

Major General Jacob Cox in his first book wrote, "General John Adams led his brigade, riding straight at the ditch, leaping it, and mounting the parapet, where his horse was killed astride of it, and he himself pitched headlong among Casement's men, mortally wounded."[533]

Major General Jacob Cox in his second book wrote, "Shots were fired and horse and rider fell. The horse struggled to its feet, dashed for the breastworks, leaped upon them, and fell dead astride of them. The wounded officer was Gen. John Adams. He was brought in and died."[534]

Colonel W.D. Gale, adjutant to A.P. Stewart, rode over the dreadful field of Franklin the morning after the battle, before the burial details had begun their work. He noted the bodies, piled in the ditches, "in all unseemly deformity of violent death. Gen. Adams rode his horse upon the breastworks, and both horse and rider fell there."[535]

Private M.A. Ryan of the Fourteenth Mississippi wrote, "General John Adams rode his horse on top of the enemy's breastworks. His horse was killed with his forefeet and hanging on the inside of their works. General Adams was pierced with eight Minnie balls and fell inside of their works and died in fifteen minutes with his head resting on the arms of a Federal Colonel."[536]

Private Sam R. Watkins, Company H, First Tennessee Regiment, wrote, "General Adams' horse had his fore feet on one side of the works and his hind feet on the other, dead. The general seems to have been caught so that he was held to the horse's back, sitting almost as if living, riddled and mangled, and torn with balls."[537]

Appendix C

Tributes

Colonel James R. Binford served with General Adams and wrote a letter to Adams's sister Martha: "Gen. Adams was a kingly man without the royalty usually attached to that class. He was a true type of the American or rather Southern, soldier—ever modest, conservative, brave, and patriotic. He seemed not to know fear. To do his duty at all times and under all circumstances was ever his desire. No truer or braver officer ever gave his life in defense of his beloved Southland." Later he wrote, "History has never done him justice."[538]

Captain John Collins wrote, "As a man, Gen. Adams was greatly above the ordinary in every sense, and a true friend of mine to the last."[539]

Dr. Charles Todd Quintard traveled with the Southern armies as a chaplain. He became an Episcopal bishop. He was with the army as it marched to Franklin. After the battle, he recalled John Adams this way:

> *As a soldier, General Adams was active, calm and self-possessed, brave without rashness, quick to perceive and ever ready to seize the favorable moment. He enjoyed the confidence of his superiors and the love and respect of his soldiers and officers. In camp and on the march he looked closely to the comfort of his soldiers, and often shared his horse on long marches with his sick and broken-down men.... There is no shadow on his memory and he left to his children the heritage of an unblemished name and to coming generations the sublime heroism of a Southern Soldier.*[540]

Alexander Peter "A.P." Stewart wrote a lengthy recollection of Adams at Franklin, which included this:

> *At Franklin, there was not a more natural or sublime display of true heroism than was made by Brigadier General John Adams, a Tennessean, commanding a brigade in Loring's division, Stewart's corps. It was natural because it emanated spontaneously from one whose very nature was heroic and who, consequently, could not act otherwise than heroically.*[541]

The former Federal officer who approached the table of Southerners at the banquet in Louisville, Kentucky, whose name Governor James D. Porter could not recall, said:

> *I watched him as he led his brigade against our works. He looked like a soldier inspired with the belief that the fortunes of his cause depended upon his own actions; and when his horse leaped upon our works for one moment there was a cessation of firing, caused no doubt, by admiration of his lofty courage. Another moment, as he called to his command to follow, a volley was delivered and rider and horse fell dead inside of our works.*

Left: A bust of John Adams at the Vicksburg battlefield commemorating his role in the Vicksburg Campaign. *Photo by author.*

Right: Adams monument on Winstead Hill along the Generals' Walk. Note the "Bonnie Blue Flag" at the top. *Photo by Randy Duncan.*

And Porter himself said, "I have long been of the opinion that the conduct of Gen. John Adams at the battle of Franklin was the most gallant action of the war."[542]

Federal officer John Casement, who opposed Adams at Franklin, wrote to Mrs. Adams, "Would that I had the power to return the gallant rider! There was not a man in my command that witnessed the gallant ride that did not express his admiration of the rider and wish that he might have lived long enough to wear the honors that he so gallantly won."[543]

Besides these written tributes to John Adams, there are monuments to him that you can visit today.

At the Vicksburg National Battlefield, across from the Tennessee Monument, there is a bust of John Adams. The plaque on the pedestal tells of his service record.

There is a bust of John Adams at the Carter House in Franklin, alongside the likenesses of the other generals killed during the battle.

Beside his grave in Pulaski, alongside the narrow walkway, there is a small marker that talks about his career.

And there is a monument to John Adams on Winstead Hill. The inscription provides the reader with a few details about his life and career. At the top of the monument is the Bonnie Blue Flag.

Appendix D

The Ring

In October 2014, forty or fifty Adamses from all over the country gathered in Franklin, Tennessee, for a family reunion and to mark the 150th anniversary of the Battle of Franklin. I was fortunate enough to be invited as an "honorary cousin" since I had been researching their famous ancestor. During the course of the weekend, I got to know some of them, including Lawrence "Larry" Adams. Larry and his lovely wife, Nancy, had come from Florissant, Missouri, to attend. Larry is General Adams's great-grandson. Larry's grandfather was the General's namesake, John Adams.

One of the events of that weekend was a bus tour that started in Spring Hill and followed the General's route to Franklin. We were honored to have as our tour guide renowned Civil War historian (and genuinely nice guy) Thomas Cartwright. The tour stopped at Rippavilla, and we were waiting around for the next event. Thomas, Larry and I were standing at the railing on the second floor, overlooking the stairs. Larry said something to me about a ring that had been handed down to him from his father and how he wished he knew more about it. Thomas asked if it was a wedding ring, and Larry said, no, it has an "A" on it. Thomas said it was too bad it wasn't a wedding ring because one of the Federal officers had sent the ring to Mrs. Adams after it had been taken from the General's dead body. I jumped in and said, "Wait a minute, the officer never said it was a wedding ring." I turned to Larry and asked, "Larry, is that ring kind of square or kind of oval?" Larry thought for a minute and replied, "Kind of oval."

Left: The ring John Adams was likely wearing the night he was killed. *Photo by Nancy Adams.*

Below: Lawrence "Larry" Adams at his great-grandfather's (General Adams) grave in Pulaski, Tennessee. *Photo by author.*

If you take a close look at the photograph of John and Georgiana Adams, it's almost as if he wants us to see the large ring on his right hand. The ring in the photo is oval-shaped with a large stone. The ring in Larry's possession is oval-shaped and has a large stone that is engraved with the letter "A." We have had experts look at the ring. Unfortunately, because the photo does not allow us to see whether it is inscribed, there is so far no way to absolutely confirm that Larry's ring is the same one.

Federals sent John Adams's ring to Georgiana not long after the Battle of Franklin was over. Larry's grandfather was the son named after the General. The ring has been handed down from father to son. Taking these facts into consideration along with the photograph, the experts agreed that it most likely is the same ring.

The day after the big reunion, a small group of us drove to the cemetery in Pulaski, Tennessee, where General Adams is buried. We were honored to have former Pulaski mayor Dan Speer meet us there and give a talk on the history of the town. Jeanne Crawford made the drive down, as did Thomas Patton Adams. The three of us have worked for many years on this project, and there we were, all together, standing in that quiet place. Larry Adams was there also. The Adamses left and were going to meet somewhere local for lunch. They invited me, but I felt that was family time, and so we departed, perhaps forever.

I hope this book is pleasing to them, and to the General and his beautiful wife, Georgiana. And I hope that that ring stays in the possession of the Adams family and continues to be handed down as a reminder of a very brave man, John Adams, a Tennessee hero.

Notes

Preface

1. Gibson letter to Adams.
2. Tennessee State Museum.

Chapter 1

3. "Gen John Adams at Franklin: Testimony," 299–302; *Courier-Journal*, December 1, 1881.

Chapter 2

4. Crawford, "Adams and Eldridge Brief Sketches"; Gilbert and Gilbert, *True for the Cause of Liberty*, 22–28.
5. Cowles collection, obituary of Mrs. Martha Adams.
6. Crawford, "Adams and Eldridge Brief Sketches."
7. Carter House Folder, Nathan Adams article.
8. Philadelphia Directory and Register of 1813, 1816 and 1817.
9. *Poulson's American Daily Advertiser*, January 10, 1817.
10. Crawford, "Adams and Eldridge Brief Sketches."
11. Adams, "Adams Family History."

12. Crawford, "Adams and Eldridge Brief Sketches"; Adams, "Family History"; *Nashville Clarion*, September 2, 1817.
13. Carter House Folder, Nathan Adams article.
14. Andrew Jackson papers, Library of Congress.
15. Cowles collection, obituary of Mrs. Martha Adams.
16. Crawford, "Adams and Eldridge Brief Sketches."
17. Ibid.
18. Lucas, *Marriage Records Book.*
19. Adams, "Biography of a Frontier American," 14.
20. Goodstein, *Nashville*, 1–2.
21. Ibid., 21.
22. Ibid., 117–18.
23. Hoss and Reese, "History of Nashville," 102–3.
24. Remini, *Andrew Jackson*, 74–75.
25. Hoss and Reese, "History of Nashville," 102–3.

Chapter 3

26. *Nashville Whig*, July 2, 1825.
27. Hoobler, *Cities Under the Gun*, 72.
28. Davidson County General Index to Deeds.
29. Crawford, "Adams and Eldridge Brief Sketches."
30. *Memphis Daily Appeal*, November 13, 1873.
31. *Memphis Daily Avalanche*, Tuesday, October 9, 1860.
32. Gibson, "Maj. Thomas P. Adams," 420; Burrow, *Arlington*, 59.
33. The Hermitage Collection, invitation to a Ball for President-Elect Andrew Jackson.
34. Texas State Historical Association, "William Harris Wharton."
35. The Hermitage Collection, invitation to a Ball for President-Elect Andrew Jackson.
36. Remini, *Andrew Jackson*, 150–53.
37. Hoss and Reese, "History of Nashville," 280.
38. Ibid., 283–84.
39. "Gen John Adams at Franklin: Testimony," 299–302.
40. Giles County General Index to Deeds.

Chapter 4

41. Cox, "Turnpikes and Bridges."
42. Friends of Metropolitan Archives of Nashville, "Nashville Archives."

Chapter 5

43. Adams, "Biography of a Frontier American," 18.
44. Christoff letter to author, John Adams, Department of the Army Applications papers.
45. Ibid.
46. Ibid.
47. Ibid.
48. Giles County Chancery Court file A15 court case 3099.
49. *Times Picayune*, "Life Insurance—A Case in Point," May 14, 1841.

Chapter 6

50. Waugh, *Class of 1846*, 7.
51. Ibid., 8.
52. Ibid., 9.
53. Ibid., 14–15.
54. Ibid., 15–16.
55. Ibid., 18–25.
56. Ibid., 19.
57. Official Register, West Point, John Adams.
58. Ibid.
59. Ibid.
60. Waugh, *Class of 1846*, 23–24.

Chapter 7

61. San Diego Historical Society, "Cave Johnson Couts."
62. Cave Couts letters, Huntington Library.
63. Official Register, West Point, John Adams.
64. Waugh, *Class of 1846*, 38.

65. Ibid., 39.
66. Official Register, West Point, John Adams.
67. Waugh, *Class of 1846*, 44.
68. Cave Couts letters, Huntington Library.
69. Ibid.
70. Waugh, *Class of 1846*, 29.
71. Cave Couts letters, Huntington Library.
72. Ibid.
73. Waugh, *Class of 1846*, 50.
74. Cowley and Guinzburg, *West Point*, 258.
75. Waugh, *Class of 1846*, 51.
76. Cave Couts letters, Huntington Library.
77. Official Register, West Point, John Adams.
78. Waugh, *Class of 1846*, 62–64.
79. Ibid., xiv–xvi.
80. Ibid., 17.

Chapter 8

81. Waugh, *Class of 1846*, 58.
82. Adams, "Biography of a Frontier American," 25.
83. Hyslop, *Bound for Santa Fe*, 1–12; Merry, *A Country of Vast Designs*, 239–41; Campbell, *Gone to Texas*, 94.
84. Singletary, *Mexican War*, 10–11.
85. Merry, *A Country of Vast Designs*, 241.
86. Singletary, *Mexican War*, 13.

Chapter 9

87. Sides, *Blood and Thunder*, 56, 67.
88. Ibid., 18–21; Groom, *Kearney's March*, 65.
89. Adams, "Biography of a Frontier American," 31.
90. Government Printing Office, *List of Staff Officers of the Confederate States Army*, 3.
91. Adams, "Biography of a Frontier American," 31–32.
92. National Park Service, "Dragoon Soldier."
93. State of Missouri Historical Society, "Sterling Price."

94. Gorenfeld, "Battle of Santa Cruz de Rosales" and "Letter: Cave Couts to John Love."
95. Texas State Historical Association, "Benjamin Lloyd Beall."
96. William L. Clements Library, "John Love Papers."
97. Adams, "Biography of a Frontier American," 34–35.
98. Ibid., 35–36.
99. Gorenfeld, "Battle of Santa Cruz de Rosales."
100. Ibid.
101. Ibid.
102. Ibid.
103. Ibid.
104. Ibid.
105. Ibid.
106. Gorenfeld, letter to author.
107. Ibid.
108. Adams, "Biography of a Frontier American," 41.
109. Gorenfeld, letter to author.
110. Adams, "Biography of a Frontier American," 41.
111. Gorenfeld, letter to author.

Chapter 10

112. Adams, "Biography of a Frontier American," 41–42.
113. Gorenfeld, "Letter: Cave Couts to John Love."
114. Ibid.
115. Adams, "Biography of a Frontier American," 41–43.
116. Ibid., 43–44.
117. Ibid., 44–46.
118. John Adams letter to George Cullum.
119. National Park Service, "Dragoon Soldier."
120. Gorenfeld, "Letter: Cave Couts to John Love."
121. National Park Service, "Dragoon Soldier."

Chapter 11

122. Adams, "Biography of a Frontier American," 43–47.
123. Cullum, *Biographical Register of the Officers and Graduates*.

124. Adams, "Biography of a Frontier American," 48.
125. Sides, *Blood and Thunder*, 5–8.
126. National Park Service, "Places to Go in New Mexico."
127. Sides, *Blood and Thunder*, 50.
128. Ibid., 53–54.
129. Adams, "Biography of a Frontier American," 55–56.
130. Ibid., 56–57.
131. Ibid.
132. Ibid., 57–58.
133. Ibid., 51–52.
134. Ibid., 62.
135. Ibid.
136. McDougall, "Tribute to Charles McDougall."
137. McDougall, letter to Adams.
138. McDougall, "Tribute to Charles McDougall."
139. Findagrave.com, "Georgiana McDougall Adams"; Ninth Census, 1870, City of St Louis.
140. ArlingtonNationalCemetery.net, "Thomas Mower McDougall."
141. Adams, "Biography of a Frontier American," 65.
142. McDougall, "Tribute to Charles McDougall."

Chapter 12

143. National Park Service, *Soldier and Brave*, 169–70.
144. Adams, "Biography of a Frontier American," 67.
145. Ibid., 70.
146. Ibid., 71.
147. Ibid., 71–73.
148. Ibid., 74–75.

Chapter 13

149. Green, *Five Years a Dragoon*, 157.
150. Adams, "Biography of a Frontier American," 76.
151. Green, *Five Years a Dragoon*, 157–64.
152. Catton, *Army of the Potomac*, 113.
153. Frazer, *Forts of the West*, 105.

154. Ibid., 76.
155. Michno, *Encyclopedia of Indian Wars*, 22–27.
156. Frazer, *Forts of the West*, 98.
157. Guild and Carter, *Kit Carson*, 204–5.
158. Utley, *Fort Union National Monument*, 16; Guild and Carter, *Kit Carson*, 204–5.
159. Adams, "Biography of a Frontier American," 77–78.
160. Michno, *Encyclopedia of Indian Wars*, 32.
161. Ibid.
162. Ibid., 33.
163. Ibid.
164. Adams, "Biography of a Frontier American," 81.
165. Ibid., 80.
166. Ibid., 81.
167. Ibid., 82–83.
168. Ibid., 83.

Chapter 14

169. Adams, "Biography of a Frontier American," 84–85.
170. Ibid., 84.
171. Green, *Five Years a Dragoon*, 6.
172. Ibid., 7.
173. Ibid., 8.
174. Adams, "Biography of a Frontier American," 97.
175. Ibid., 88.
176. Ibid., 86.
177. Ibid., 88.
178. Chancery Court, Giles County, Tennessee, File A15, court case 3099.
179. Ibid.
180. Ibid.
181. Ibid.
182. Ibid.; e-mail from researcher Marsha Smith with various documents regarding Maurice Cleveland.
183. Adams, "Biography of a Frontier American," 88.

Chapter 15

184. Adams, transcribed letters, letter of January 17, 1859.
185. American Pacific Line, "Travel Times New York to San Francisco."
186. Pederson, "San Francisco History."
187. Adams, transcribed letters, letter of January 17, 1859.
188. Fort Crook Historical Society, "Fort Crook Museum."
189. Adams, transcribed letters, letter of January 20, 1859.
190. Ibid.
191. Ibid., March 12, 1859.
192. Ibid.
193. Ibid., July 31, 1859.
194. Ibid., May 10, 1859.
195. Ibid., June 14, 1859.
196. Ibid., August 10, 1859.
197. Ibid.
198. Adams, "Biography of a Frontier American," 100–2.
199. Ibid., 102–3.
200. Adams, transcribed letters, letter of August 22, 1859.
201. Ibid., September 14, 1859.
202. Ibid., October 14, 1859.
203. Adams, "Biography of a Frontier American," 104–5.
204. Adams, transcribed letters, letter of December 28, 1859.
205. McDougall, "Tribute to Charles McDougall."
206. U.S. War Department, *War of the Rebellion* (hereafter OR), ser. 1, vol. 50, part 1, 451.
207. McDougall, "Tribute to Charles McDougall."
208. OR, ser. 1, vol. 50, part 1, 466.
209. Adams, "Biography of a Frontier American," 116.
210. OR, ser. 1, vol. 50, part 1, 486.
211. Ibid., 526.
212. Ibid.
213. San Diego Historical Society, "Cave Johnson Couts."
214. Adams, transcribed letters, letter of May 31, 1861.

Chapter 16

215. OR, ser. 2, vol. 2, 38.

216. *Nashville Federal and American*, Saturday, August 10, 1861.
217. Adams, "Biography of a Frontier American," 121.
218. Crawford, "Adams and Eldridge Brief Sketches."
219. Blueandgrayeducation.org, "Story in Warfighting."
220. Hardison, "St. John's Episcopal Church."
221. Mocivilwar150.com, "Missouri Civil War Sesquicentennial."
222. *Memphis Daily Appeal*, November 15, 1861.
223. OR, ser. 2, vol. 3, 744.
224. Ibid., 772.
225. Ibid., ser. 2, vol. 1, 546.
226. Crawford, "Adams and Eldridge Brief Sketches."
227. John Adams Military Service, Record National Archives.
228. National Park Service, "Fort Donelson."
229. American Heritage, *American Heritage Book of the Presidents*, 481–82.
230. Catton, *American Heritage Picture History of the Civil War*, 118–19.
231. OR, ser. 2, vol. 3, 803.
232. Adams, "Biography of a Frontier American," 121–24.
233. Ibid., 122.
234. Ibid., 124.

Chapter 17

235. Adams, "Biography of a Frontier American," 127.
236. OR, ser. 1, vol. 3, 305.
237. Ibid., ser. 1, vol. 52, part 2, 127–28.
238. Ibid., ser. 1, vol. 3, 306.
239. CivilWarReference.com, "George Hollins."
240. OR, ser. 1, vol. 19, part 1, 379–81.
241. Sword, *Shiloh*, 97, 108, 270–72.
242. Young, *To the Tyrants Never Yield*, 94.
243. Adams, "Biography of a Frontier American," 129.

Chapter 18

244. Ibid.
245. Ibid., 129–30.
246. Ibid., 130.

247. Rorer, "Noble Martyrs in a Holy Cause."
248. OR, ser. 1, vol. 10, part 1, 887.
249. Adams, "Biography of a Frontier American," 131.
250. Ibid., 132.
251. Ibid., 132–34.
252. Ibid., 134.
253. TerrysTexasRangers.org, "John Austin Wharton."
254. Nesbitt Memorial Library, "Diary of James T. Pettus."
255. Adams, "Biography of a Frontier American," 134–3; OR, ser. 1, vol. 10, part 1, 895–96.
256. Young, *To the Tyrants Never Yield*, 184–85.
257. TerrysTexasRangers.org, "John Austin Wharton."
258. Adams, "Biography of a Frontier American," 135.

Chapter 19

259. OR, ser. 1, vol. 10, part 2, 397.
260. Raulston and Livingood, *Sequatchie*, 141.
261. LancasteratWar.com, "Battle of Sweeden's Cove."
262. Ibid.
263. Adams, "Biography of a Frontier American," 136.
264. LancasteratWar.com, "Battle of Sweeden's Cove."
265. Ibid.
266. OR, ser. 1, vol. 10, part 1, 903–5.
267. Ibid.
268. LancasteratWar.com, "Battle of Sweeden's Cove."
269. OR, ser. 1, vol. 10, part 1, 904.
270. Ibid., 905.
271. Ibid., 920.
272. Ibid., ser. 2, vol. 5, 510.
273. Adams, "Biography of a Frontier American," 138.

Chapter 20

274. Ibid.
275. "Capt Thomas Gibson," 80.
276. Hoss and Reese, "History of Nashville."

277. Ibid.
278. Ibid.
279. OR, ser. 1, vol. 17, part 2, 666–69.
280. Ibid.
281. Catton, *American Heritage Picture History of the Civil War*, 242.
282. Ibid., 245.
283. OR, ser. 1, vol. 17, part 2, 740.
284. Ibid., 758.
285. Adams, "Biography of a Frontier American," 140–44.
286. OR, ser. 1, vol. 17, part 2, 797.
287. Ibid., 798.
288. Ibid., 799.
289. Ibid., 817–19.
290. Ibid.
291. Ibid., 826.

Chapter 21

292. Adams, Military Service Record.
293. Catton, *American Heritage Picture History of the Civil War*, 266; Woodworth, *Jefferson Davis and His Generals*, 170.
294. Adams, Military Service Record.
295. Ibid.
296. Ibid.
297. Ibid.
298. OR, ser. 1, vol. 24, part 1, 216.
299. "American Memory: A History of Lawmaking."

Chapter 22

300. OR, ser. 1, vol. 24, part 3, 611.
301. Ibid., 609.
302. Ibid., 613.
303. Adams, "Biography of a Frontier American," 148.
304. Ibid., 149.
305. OR, ser. 1, vol. 24, part 3, 647.
306. Ibid., 807.

307. Collins, "Mississippi and Kentucky in a Contest," 460.
308. Collins, "Gallant Mike Farrell," 372–75.
309. "Surgeons of the Confederacy," 336–37.

Chapter 23

310. Adams, "Biography of a Frontier American," 151–52.
311. OR, ser. 1, vol. 24, part 1, 532.
312. Ibid., ser. 1, vol. 24, part 3, 785.
313. Ibid., ser. 1, vol. 24, part 1, 531.
314. Ibid., ser. 1, vol. 24, part 1, 532.
315. Adams, "Biography of a Frontier American," 152
316. Catton, *American Heritage Picture History of the Civil War*, 315.
317. Adams, "Biography of a Frontier American," 154.
318. OR, ser. 1, vol. 24, part 3, 822.
319. Ibid., 845.
320. Ibid., 850.
321. Ibid.
322. Ibid., 853.
323. Ibid., 859.
324. Ibid., 860.
325. Bearss, *Decision in Mississippi*, 305–6.
326. Grabau, *Ninety-Eight Days*, 464.
327. OR, ser. 1, vol. 24, part 3, 870.
328. Ibid.
329. Ibid., 878.
330. Ibid., 881.
331. Bearss, *Decision in Mississippi*, 310–11.
332. Ibid., 309.

Chapter 24

333. niu.edu, "Mechanicsburg Diary."
334. Bearss, *Decision in Mississippi*, 234.
335. Ibid., 241.
336. Ibid., 244.
337. Bearss, *Decision in Mississippi*, 341.

338. Belcher, *Eleventh Missouri Volunteer Infantry*, 133.
339. Grabau, *Ninety-Eight Days*, 464–65.
340. OR, ser. 1, vol. 24, part 2, 430, 441–42.
341. Ibid., ser. 1, vol. 24, part 1, 442.
342. Ibid.
343. Bearss, *Decision in Mississippi*, 360.
344. Ibid.
345. OR, ser. 1, vol. 24, part 3, 955.

Chapter 25

346. Ibid., 1040.
347. Rorer, "Noble Martyrs in a Holy Cause."
348. Ancestry.com, applications for U.S. passports, 1795–1925, Emma Portis Adams Dickson (accessed by researcher Marsha Smith, November 15, 2016, scanned copy in possession of author).
349. Adams, "Biography of a Frontier American," 160.
350. Ibid., 62.

Chapter 26

351. Sword, *Embrace an Angry Wind*, 27.
352. Ibid., 26.
353. Bonds, *War Like the Thunderbolt*, 12.
354. Adams, "Biography of a Frontier American," 163.
355. Connelly, *Autumn of Glory*, 339.
356. Ibid., 340.
357. Jones and Martin, *Gentle Rebel*, 26.
358. Connelly, *Autumn of Glory*, 342–43.
359. Ibid., 27.
360. Adams, "Biography of a Frontier American," 163–65.
361. Connelly, *Autumn of Glory*, 358.
362. Rowland, *Military History of Mississippi*, 240.
363. Connelly, *Autumn of Glory*, 358.
364. Catton, *American Heritage Picture History of the Civil War*, 478.
365. Connelly, *Autumn of Glory*, 359.
366. Ibid.

367. Jones and Martin, *Gentle Rebel*, 32–39.
368. Sword, *Embrace an Angry Wind*, 40.
369. Jones and Martin, *Gentle Rebel*, 46–49.
370. Bonds, *War Like the Thunderbolt*, 14.
371. Woodworth, *Jefferson Davis and His Generals*, 177–78, 216.
372. Sword, *Embrace an Angry Wind*, 27.
373. Jones and Martin, *Gentle Rebel*, 57–58.
374. Wiley, *Life of Johnny Reb*, 241.
375. Woodworth, *Jefferson Davis and His Generals*, 283, 285.

Chapter 27

376. Buckhead Heritage Society, "Moore's Mill."
377. McMurry, *Atlanta 1864*, 147–49.
378. Buckhead Heritage Society, "Moore's Mill."
379. OR, ser. 1, vol. 38, part 3, 891–92.
380. Ibid., 893–94.
381. Jones and Martin, *Gentle Rebel*, 60–61.
382. Ibid., 63.
383. Ibid., 64–71.
384. Woodworth, *Jefferson Davis and His Generals*, 288.
385. Bonds, *War Like the Thunderbolt*, 279–82.
386. Ibid., 91.
387. Catton, *American Heritage Picture History of the Civil War*, 526.
388. Bonds, *War Like the Thunderbolt*, 111.

Chapter 28

389. Jacobson and Rupp, *For Cause and for Country*, 34–42.
390. "Heroism at Franklin," 457–58.
391. Henry, "Adams's Brigade," 76–77.
392. Jones and Martin, *Gentle Rebel*, 107.

Chapter 29

393. Seabrook, *Encyclopedia of the Battle of Franklin*, appendix B, 354; Sword, *Embrace an Angry Wind*, 444–46.
394. Seabrook, *Encyclopedia of the Battle of Franklin*, 358.
395. Cartwright, interview with author.
396. Rowland, *Military History of Mississippi*, 231.
397. Ibid., 170–78.
398. Ibid., 220–26.
399. Ibid., 228–34.
400. Ibid., 235–41.
401. Ibid., 253.
402. Ibid., 351–54.

Chapter 30

403. Civilwarhome.com, "Journal of the Army of Tennessee."
404. Jones and Martin, *Gentle Rebel*, 114.
405. *Professional Papers of the Corps of Engineers*, 213–28.
406. Niepert, "Civil War Pontoon Bridges."
407. "Heroism at Franklin," 457–58.
408. Rorer, "Noble Martyrs in a Holy Cause."

Chapter 31

409. Carter House Folder.
410. Sword, *Embrace an Angry Wind*, 88.
411. Jacobson and Rupp, *For Cause and for Country*, 55.
412. Jones and Martin, *Gentle Rebel*, 116.
413. Ibid.
414. Sword, *Embrace an Angry Wind*, 89.
415. Jones and Martin, *Gentle Rebel*, 115–16.
416. Carter House Folder.
417. Jones and Martin, *Gentle Rebel*, 117.
418. Carter House Folder.
419. Jones and Martin, *Gentle Rebel*, 117.
420. Civilwarhome.com, "Journal of the Army of Tennessee."

421. Jones and Martin, *Gentle Rebel*, 117.
422. Civilwarhome.com, "Journal of the Army of Tennessee."
423. Jones and Martin, *Gentle Rebel*, 117.
424. Carter House Folder.
425. Government Printing Office, *List of Staff Officers of the Confederate States Army*, 3.
426. Jones and Martin, *Gentle Rebel*, 117.
427. Ibid., 118; Civilwarhome.com, "Journal of the Army of Tennessee."
428. Watkins, *Co. Aytch*, 227.
429. Seabrook, *Encyclopedia of the Battle of Franklin*, 276–77.
430. Carter House Folder.
431. Jones and Martin, *Gentle Rebel*, 118; Jacobson and Rupp, *For Cause and for Country*, 74.
432. Sword, *Embrace an Angry Wind*, 97–98.
433. Elliott, *Doctor Quintard*, 190.
434. Jacobson and Rupp, *For Cause and for Country*, 102.
435. Cartwright, interview with author.
436. Sword, *Embrace an Angry Wind*, 117.
437. Cartwright, interview with author.
438. Jacobson and Rupp, *For Cause and for Country*, 151.
439. Cartwright, interview with author; Sword, *Embrace an Angry Wind*, 137–39.
440. Sword, *Embrace an Angry Wind*, 114–55.

Chapter 32

441. Sword, *Embrace an Angry Wind*, 158, 177.
442. Jones and Martin, *Gentle Rebel*, 122.
443. Sword, *Embrace an Angry Wind*, 177.
444. Seabrook, *Encyclopedia of the Battle of Franklin*, 365–75.
445. Ibid., 229–30.
446. Rorer, "Noble Martyrs in a Holy Cause."
447. Bonds, *War Like the Thunderbolt*, 47, 295–96.
448. Sword, *Embrace an Angry Wind*, 177.
449. Seabrook, *Encyclopedia of the Battle of Franklin*, 208; Sword, *Embrace an Angry Wind*, 216.
450. Sword, *Embrace an Angry Wind*, 178.
451. Ibid., 179.

452. Fraley, "Major General W.W. Loring's Confederate Division."
453. Mason, "Osage Orange."
454. Cartwright, interview with author.
455. Fraley, "Major General W.W. Loring's Confederate Division"; Sword, *Embrace an Angry Wind*, 215; Cartwright, interview with author.
456. Sword, *Embrace an Angry Wind*, 214–15.
457. Logsdon, *Eyewitnesses at the Battle of Franklin*, 20.
458. Sword, *Embrace an Angry Wind*, 215–16.
459. Edwards, *Civil War Guns*, 158–62.
460. "Heroism at Franklin," 457–58.
461. Ibid., 457; Rorer, "Noble Martyrs in a Holy Cause."
462. Cartwright, interview with author.
463. Logsdon, *Eyewitnesses at the Battle of Franklin*, 8.
464. Sword, *Embrace an Angry Wind*, 186–87.
465. Woodworth, *Jefferson Davis and His Generals*, 300.
466. "Gen John Adams at Franklin: Testimony," 299–302.
467. Thomas Gibson, *The Tennessean*, April 5, 1901.
468. Logsdon, *Eyewitnesses at the Battle of Franklin*, 8–9.
469. Union Pacific, "Significant Individuals," "General John Stephen 'Jack' Casement."
470. Sword, *Embrace an Angry Wind*, 214–16.
471. Ibid., 216.
472. Jones and Martin, *Gentle Rebel*, 122.
473. Logsdon, *Eyewitnesses at the Battle of Franklin*, 19.
474. "Gen John Adams at Franklin: Testimony," 299–302.
475. Logsdon, *Eyewitnesses at the Battle of Franklin*, 27.
476. Fraley, interview with author.
477. Collins, "Gallant Mike Farrell," 372–75.
478. Henry, "Adams's Brigade," 76–77.
479. Jacobson and Rupp, *For Cause and for Country*, 361.
480. Sword, *Embrace an Angry Wind*, 226.
481. *The Tennessean*, Friday April 5, 1901.
482. "Heroism at Franklin," 457–58.
483. Stevens, "Other Side in Battle of Franklin," 165–68.
484. "Particulars of Gen John Adams's Death," 482–83; Field, *Bright Skies and Dark Shadows*, 252; McDonough and Connelly, *Five Tragic Hours*, 147.
485. "Gens. Cleburne and Adams at Franklin," 154–55.
486. Stevens, "Other Side in Battle of Franklin," 165–68.
487. BattleofFranklinTrust.com, "Carter House History."

488. Seabrook, *Encyclopedia of the Battle of Franklin*, 465.
489. Field, *Bright Skies and Dark Shadows*, 253.
490. "Gen John Adams at Franklin: Testimony," 299–302.
491. Lane, "Familiar Road," 46.

Chapter 33

492. Seabrook, *Encyclopedia of the Battle of Franklin*, 186.
493. Sword, *Embrace an Angry Wind*, 256–57.
494. Watkins, *Co. Aytch*, 233.
495. Sword, *Embrace an Angry Wind*, 425; McDonough and Connelly, *Five Tragic Hours*, 156.
496. Cartwright, interview with author.
497. Fraley, "Major General W.W. Loring's Confederate Division."
498. Collins, "Gallant Mike Farrell," 372–75.
499. Seabrook, *Encyclopedia of the Battle of Franklin*, 396; Noll, *Dr. Quintard*, 114; *The Tennessean*, Friday April 5, 1901.

Chapter 34

500. McDougall, letter to Adams.

Chapter 35

501. "Helen Plane," 85–86.
502. Freeman, *Carved in Stone*, 56–57.
503. "Mrs. Plane's Address of Welcome," 376–77.
504. Crutchfield, *Tennesseans at War*, 86.
505. Waldren, "Death of Gen. Felix K. Zollicoffer."
506. Hughes and Hughes, *Quiet Places*, 9–10.
507. Ibid., 33–34.
508. "Lee Memorial Day," 44.

Chapter 36

509. Warwick, *Williamson*, 85–87.

Appendix A

510. *Necrologies* 20, 65.
511. Marquis, *Book of St. Louisans*, 15.
512. *Railway Journal* 19, 12.
513. Gulbransen, various entries related to Adams family history.
514. *Anaconda Standard*, Tuesday, October 17, 1905.
515. Gulbransen, various entries related to Adams family history; Cox, "Family History."
516. Parker, *Records of the Association of Acting Assistant Surgeons of the United States*, 13.
517. Find a Grave, "Mary Margaret Adams."
518. *Journal Lancet* 40, 353.
519. *Necrologies* 14, 136; Gulbransen, various entries related to Adams family history.
520. Gulbransen, various entries related to Adams family history; Ancestry.com, U.S. Passport Applications, 1795–1925, Emma Portis Adams Dickson.
521. St. Louis Society Scrapbook, 1889–1906, 26.
522. *The Tennessean*, May 4, 1890.
523. *St. Louis Dispatch*, December 12, 1905.

Appendix B

524. Elliott, *Doctor Quintard*, 191.
525. *The Tennessean*, April 5, 1901.
526. "Gen John Adams at Franklin: Testimony," 299–302.
527. Ibid., 301.
528. Jacobson and Rupp, *For Cause and for Country*, 364.
529. "Death and Identity of Gen. Adams," 264.
530. Ibid.
531. "Gens. Cleburne and Adams at Franklin," 154–55.
532. Stevens, "Other Side in Battle of Franklin," 165–68.

533. Cox, *Campaigns of the Civil War*, 91.
534. "Particulars of Gen John Adams's Death," 482.
535. Ibid., 483.
536. Fraley, "Major General W.W. Loring's Confederate Division."
537. Watkins, *Co. Aytch*, 235.

Appendix C

538. "Heroism at Franklin," 457–58.
539. Ibid., 458.
540. Noll, *Doctor Quintard*, 114–15.
541. Seabrook, *Encyclopedia of the Battle of Franklin*, 462–63.
542. "Gen. Adams at Franklin," 302.
543. Ibid., 301.

Bibliography

Primary Sources

Adams, John. Application Papers, including letters of recommendations of Aaron V. Brown, and statements from Adams's teachers and information related to Adams's demerits. Department of the Army, United States Military Academy, West Point, NY. Suzanne Christoff, archivist, United States Military Academy, letter to author March 22, 1993, USMA. (Copies in possession of author.)

———. Letters to George Cullum, February 6, 1860, and April 25, 1860. Judith Sibley, West Point Manuscript Librarian. Department of the Army, United States Military Academy, West Point, NY, June 16, 1993, letter to author. (Copies in possession of author.)

———. Military Service Record. National Archives. Letters related to John Adams nomination to Brigadier General. (Copies in possession of author.)

———. Transcribed letters, National Archives, Fort Crook Letters RG: 393, Pt.V, Stack: 9W2, 13/07/02. Fort Crook Letters Sent, Vol. 1, entire volume. Keith Arnold. June 2002.

Census Records, City of St. Louis. St. Louis County, MO. Ward 7. 1870.

Couts, Cave. Letters from John Adams. Henry E. Huntington Library, San Marino, CA. (Copies in possession of author.)

Davidson County, Tennessee records. General Index to Deeds, 1784–1871.

Gibson, Thomas. Letter to Mary E. Adams of Arlington, dated October 1901. (Copy in possession of author.)

Giles County, Tennessee records. General Index to Deeds, 1810–1859, and Chancery Court File A15 Court Case 3099.

Gorenfeld, Will, ed. Author of Musketoon Website. Copies of dispatches related to the Battle of Santa Cruz de Rosales. Letter to author. (Copies in possession of author.)

Library of Congress, Andrew Jackson Papers.

Macpherson, Sharon, curator of research, The Hermitage, Nashville, TN. Letter to T. Patton Adams, December 6, 1989, regarding a ball in Nashville for Andrew Jackson.

McDougall, Charles. Letter to Anne Tennant Adams, Philadelphia, PA, February 14, 1865. Jeanne Crawford, November 2007, letter to author.

Ninth Census, 1870. Population Schedule, City of St. Louis. St. Louis County, MO, Ward 7, p. 685, Dwelling 576, Family 720, Lines 21–32, 1870.

Official Register. Officers and Cadets of the U.S. Military Academy. West Point, NY, June 1842–June 1846. Suzanne Christoff, archivist, United States Military Academy, letter to author March 22, 1993, USMA. (Copies in possession of author.)

Philadelphia Register and Directory of 1813, 1816 and 1817.

Pilgrim, Michael E. Military Reference Branch, Textual Reference Division, National Archives letter to author. July 1, 1993. No known record of Adams's physical characteristics.

Rorer, Walter A. "Noble Martyrs in a Holy Cause." The Civil War Letters of Walter A. Rorer, Capt./Maj./Lt.-Col., 20th Mississippi Infantry, CSA. From the James M. Willcox Papers, "Records of Ante-Bellum Southern Plantation Records from the Revolution through the Civil War." Rare Book, Manuscript and Special Collections Library, Duke University. Transcribed November 2006 by Jim Huffman, Picayune, MS, from microfilm supplied by Scott Bell, Jacksonville, TX. (Copy in possession of author.)

Tennessee State Museum. Photographs of Adams's relics and newspaper article from 1907 regarding the donation of the relics to the Tennessee Historical Society.

Interviews

Cartwright, Thomas. Historian and Audio/Video Projects, Lotz House, Franklin, TN. April 17, 2014.

Fraley, David. Curator, Carter House, Franklin, TN. March 29, 2008.
Speer, Dan, former mayor of Pulaski, TN. October 12, 2014.
White, Elizabeth. Historian, Giles County, TN. January 29, 1993.
Woodward, Margeurite. Pulaski, TN. August 15, 1993.

Newspapers and Periodicals

Anaconda Standard (Anaconda, MT), Tuesday, October 17, 1905.
Columbia Herald (Columbia, TN), December 8, 1899.
Courier-Journal (Louisville, KY), December 1, 1881.
Daily Constitutionalist (Augusta, GA), Thursday, March 16, 1865.
Memphis Daily Appeal (Memphis, TN), various dates.
Memphis Daily Avalanche (Memphis, TN), Tuesday, October 9, 1860.
Nashville Clarion (Nashville, TN), advertisement, September 2, 1817.
Nashville Federal and American (Nashville, TN), Saturday, August 10, 1861.
Nashville Gazette (Nashville, TN), advertisement, September 22, 1819.
Nashville Union and American (Nashville, TN), Saturday, August 10, 1861.
Nashville Whig (Nashville, TN), July 2, 1825.
Poulson's American Daily Advertiser (Philadelphia), Friday, January 10, 1817.
St. Louis Dispatch (St. Louis, MO), obituaries, "Pallen–Adams," February 1886.
Tennessean (Nashville, TN), Friday, April 5, 1901; Friday, December 1, 1899; May 4, 1890.
Times Picayune (New Orleans). "Life Insurance—A Case in Point." May 14, 1841.

Magazines

"The Battle of Franklin." *Confederate Veteran Magazine* 11 (1903): 166–67.
"Capt Thomas Gibson." *Confederate Veteran Magazine* 26 (1918): 80.
Collins, John L. "Gallant Mike Farrell." *Confederate Veteran Magazine* 34 (1926): 372–75.
———. "Mississippi and Kentucky in a Contest." *Confederate Veteran Magazine* 27 (1909): 460.
"Death and Identity of Gen. Adams." *Confederate Veteran Magazine* 1 (1893): 264.
Figuers, H.P. "A Boy's Impressions of the Battle of Franklin." *Confederate Veteran Magazine* 23 (1915): 4–7.

"Gen John Adams at Franklin." *Confederate Veteran Magazine* 1 (1893): 208.

"Gen John Adams at Franklin: Testimony of Union Officers to His Immutable Valor." *Confederate Veteran Magazine* 5 (1897): 299–302.

"Gens. Cleburne and Adams at Franklin." *Confederate Veteran Magazine* 10 (1902): 154–55.

Gibson, Thomas. "Maj. Thomas P. Adams." *Confederate Veteran Magazine* 9 (1901): 420.

"Helen Plane." *Confederate Veteran Magazine* 34 (1926): 85–86.

Henry, Patrick. "Adams's Brigade in Battle of Franklin." *Confederate Veteran Magazine* 21 (1913): 76–77.

"Heroism at Franklin: Tributes to Gen. Adams, Cols. Farrell and Rorke." *Confederate Veteran Magazine* 10 (1902): 457–58.

"J.L. Payne of the Thirteenth Mississippi Regiment." *Confederate Veteran Magazine* 22 (1904): 354.

Journal-Lancet 40 (1920).

Lane, Bryan. "The Familiar Road." *Civil War Times Illustrated*, October 1996.

"Lee Memorial Day." *Confederate Veteran Magazine* 32 (1924): 44.

"Make a National Park at Franklin." *Confederate Veteran Magazine* 17 (1909): 15.

McDonough, James Lee. "The Battle of Franklin Tennessee November 30, 1864." *Blue and Gray Magazine*, August/September 1984, 18–33.

Missouri Historical Society. *Necrologies* 14 (n.d.).

———. *Necrologies* 20 (September 1938–March 1940).

"Mrs. Plane's Address of Welcome." *Confederate Veteran Magazine* 3 (1895): 376–77.

"Particulars of Gen John Adams's Death." *Confederate Veteran Magazine* 22 (1904): 482–83.

Railway Journal 19 (1913).

Roberts, Frank Stovall. "Spring Hill—Franklin—Nashville—1864." *Confederate Veteran Magazine* 27 (1919): 58–59.

Stevens, Tillman H. "Other Side in Battle of Franklin." *Confederate Veteran Magazine* 2 (1903): 165–68.

"Surgeons of the Confederacy Dr. W.M. Gentry of Tennessee." *Confederate Veteran Magazine* 40 (1932): 336–37.

Books

Alderson, William T., and Robert M. McBride, eds. *Tennessee Historical Commission*. Nashville, TN: Williams Printing Company, 1965.

Ambrose, Stephen E. *Undaunted Courage: Meriwether Lewis, Thomas Jefferson, and the Opening of the American West.* New York: Simon and Schuster, 1996.

American Heritage Publishing Co. *The American Heritage Book of the Presidents and Famous Americans.* New York: American Heritage Publishing Co., 1967.

Ballard, Michael B. *John Pemberton: A Biography*. Oxford: University Press of Mississippi, 1991.

Bearss, Edwin C. *Decision in Mississippi: Mississippi's Important Role in the War Between the States.* Mississippi Commission on the War Between the States. Jackson, MS: Printed by Pioneer Press Little Rock, 1962.

Belcher, Dennis W. *The Eleventh Missouri Volunteer Infantry in the Civil War: A History and Roster.* Jefferson, NC: McFarland and Company, Inc. Publishers, 2011.

Berry, Sue, Martha Fuqua and Pam Oglesby. *Homespun Tales the Battle of Franklin.* Franklin, TN: Territorial Press, 1995.

Biographical Directory: Tennessee General Assembly 1796–1969. "Nathan Adams, 1821–1874." Tennessee State Archives.

Bonds, Russell S. *War Like the Thunderbolt: The Battle and Burning of Atlanta.* Yardley, PA: Westholme Publishing, 2010.

Bowman, Virginia McDaniel. *Historic Williamson County: Old Homes and Site.* Franklin, TN: Territorial Press, 1989.

Bromfield, Ridley. *Battles and Sketches—Army of Tennessee.* Mexico: Missouri Printing and Publishing Company, 1906.

Burrow, Rachel. *Arlington.* Arlington, TN: E.H. Clarke and Brother, 1962.

Campbell, Randolph B. *Gone to Texas: A History of the Lone Star State.* New York: Oxford University Press, 2003.

Catton, Bruce. *The Army of the Potomac: Mr. Lincoln's Army.* Garden City, NY: Doubleday and Company, 1962.

Catton, Bruce, ed. *American Heritage Picture History of the Civil War.* New York: American Heritage Publishing Co. Inc., 1960, 1982.

Cemetery Records of Giles County, Tennessee. Pulaski, TN: P-Vine Press, 1986.

Confederate Military History Extended Edition. Vol. 10, *Tennessee*. Wilmington, NC: Bradfoot Publishing Company, 1987.

Connelly, Thomas Lawrence. *Autumn of Glory: The Army of Tennessee, 1862–1865.* Baton Rouge: Louisiana State University Press, 1991.

Cowley, Robert, and Thomas Guinzburg, eds. *West Point: Two Centuries of Honor and Tradition.* New York: Warner Book, 2012.

Cox, Jacob D. *Campaigns of the Civil War: The March to the Sea—Franklin and Nashville.* Edison, NJ: Castle Books, 2002 (first published in 1882).

Crutchfield, James A. *Tennesseans at War.* Nashville, TN: Rutledge Hill Press, 1987.

Cullum, Brevet Major General George W. *Biographical Register of the Officers and Graduates of the U.S. Military Academy at West Point, New York from Its Establishment in 1802 to 1890*. 3rd ed., vol. 2, nos. 1001–2000. Boston: Houghton, Mifflin and Company, 1891. (p. 275, No. 1296, "John Adams.")

Davis, Louise Littleton. *Nashville Tales.* Gretna, LA: Pelican Publishing Company, 1981.

Davis, William C. *The Confederate General.* Vol. 1. N.p.: National Historical Society, 1992.

Dictionary of American Biographies. Vol. 1, "Abbe–Barrymore." New York: Charles Scribner's Sons, 1956.

Early Middle Tennessee Marriages. Vol. 1. Nashville, TN: Grooms, Byron Sistler and Associate, 1988.

Edwards, William B. *Civil War Guns.* Secaucus, NJ: Castle, 1982.

Elliott, Sam Davis, ed. *Doctor Quintard, Chaplain C.S.A. and Second Bishop of Tennessee: The Memoir and Civil War Diary of Charles Todd Quintard.* Baton Rouge: Louisiana State University Press, 2003.

Evans, General Clement A., ed. *Tennessee Confederate Military History.* Vol. 8. Secaucus, NJ: Blue and Grey Press, n.d.

Field, Dr. Henry M., DD. *Bright Skies and Dark Shadows*. New York: Charles Scribner's Sons, 1890.

Frazer, Robert W. *Forts of the West*. Norman: University of Oklahoma Press, 1965.

Freeman, David B. *Carved in Stone: The History of Stone Mountain.* Macon, GA: Mercer University Press, 1997.

Gilbert, Oscar E., and Catherine R. Gilbert. *True for the Cause of Liberty: The Second Spartan Regiment in the American Revolution.* Philadelphia: Casement Publishers, 2015.

Gillum, Jamie. *The Battle of Spring Hill: Twenty Five Hours…to Tragedy.* Spring Hill, TN, 2004.

Goodstein, Anita Shafer. *Nashville, 1780–1860: From Frontier to City.* Gainesville: University of Florida Press, 1989.

Gordon, Lesley J. *General George E. Pickett in Life and Legend.* Chapel Hill: University of North Carolina Press, 1998.

Government Printing Office. *List of Staff Officers of the Confederate States Army: 1861–1865.* Washington, D.C., 1891.

Grabau, Walter. *Ninety-Eight Days: A Geographer's View of the Vicksburg Campaign*. Knoxville: University of Tennessee Press, 2000.

Green, Percival. *Five Years a Dragoon ('49 to '54): And Other Adventures on the Great Plain.* Kansas City, MO: Franklin Hudson Publishing Company, 1906.

Groom, Winston. *Kearney's March: The Epic Creation of the American West, 1846–1847*. New York: Alfred A. Knopf, 2011.

Guild, Thelma S., and Harvey L. Carter. *Kit Carson: A Pattern for Heroes.* Lincoln: University of Nebraska Press, 1984

Hoobler, James A. *Cities Under the Gun: Images of Occupied Nashville and Chattanooga*. Nashville, TN: Rutledge Hill Press, 1986.

Hughes, Buckner, and Nathaniel C. Hughes. *Quiet Places: The Burial Sites of Civil War Generals in Tennessee*. N.p.: East Tennessee Historical Society, 1992.

Hyslop, Stephen G. *Bound for Santa Fe: The Road to New Mexico and the American Conquest, 1806–1848*. Norman: University of Oklahoma Press, 2002.

Jacobson, Eric A., and Richard A. Rupp. *For Cause and for Country.* Franklin, TN: O'More Publishing, 2007.

Jones, Mary Miles, and Leslie Jones Martin, eds. *The Gentle Rebel: The Civil War Letters of William Harvey Berryhill, First Lieutenant, Co. D, 43rd Regiment, Mississippi Volunteers*. Yazoo City, MS: Sassafras Press, 1982.

Key, William. *The Battle of Atlanta and the Georgia Campaign.* New York: Twayne Publishers, 1958.

Knight, James R. *Hood's Tennessee Campaign: The Desperate Venture of a Desperate Man.* Charleston, SC: The History Press, 2014.

Logsdon, David R., ed. *Eyewitnesses at the Battle of Franklin.* Nashville, TN, 1988.

Lucas, Rev. Silas Emmett, Jr. *Marriage Records, Book I, Jan. 2, 1789–Dec. 13, 1837*. Davidson County, TN: Southern Historical Press, 1979.

Marquis, Albert Nelson, ed. *The Book of St. Louisans: A Biographical Dictionary of Leading Living Men of St. Louis.* Chicago: A.N. Marquis and Company, 1912.

McDonough, James Lee, and Thomas Connelly. *Five Tragic Hours: The Battle of Franklin*. Knoxville: University of Tennessee Press, 1983.

McMurry, Richard M. *Atlanta 1864: Last Chance for the Confederacy.* Lincoln: University of Nebraska Press, 2000.

Merry, Robert W. *A Country of Vast Designs: James K. Polk, the Mexican War and the Conquest of the American Continent.* New York: Simon and Schuster, 2009.

Michno, Gregory. *Encyclopedia of Indian Wars: Western Battles and Skirmishes 1850–1890*. Missoula, MT: Mountain Press Publishing Company, 2003.

National Park Service, U.S. Department of the Interior. *Soldier and Brave: Historic Places Associated with Indian Affairs and the Indian Wars in the Trans-Mississippi West.* Honolulu, HI: University Press of the Pacific, 2005 (reprint of 1971 edition).

Noll, Arthur Howard. *Doctor Quintard Chaplain, C.S.A., and Second Bishop of Tennessee: Seeing His Story of the War (1861–1865)*. Sewanee: University Press of Sewanee, Tennessee, 1905.

Parker, W. Thornton, ed. *Records of the Association of Acting Assistant Surgeons of the United States…* Salem, MA: Salem Press Publishing and Printing, 1891.

Professional Papers of the Corps of Engineers, U.S. Army, No. 29. *Engineer Field Manual*, Parts I–VII. Washington, D.C.: Government Printing Office, 1917.

Raulston, J. Leonard, and James W. Livingood. *Sequatchie: A Story of the South Cumberlands.* Knoxville: University of Tennessee Press, 1974.

Remini, Robert V. *Andrew Jackson and the Course of American Freedom: 1822–1832.* Vol. 2. New York: Harper and Row Publishers, 1981.

Robison, Dan M. "The Carter House, Focus of the Battle of Franklin." In *Landmarks of Tennessee History*. Edited by William T. Alderson and Robert M. McBride. N.p.: Tennessee Historical Society, n.d.

Rowland, Dunbar. *Military History of Mississippi, 1803–1898*. Spartanburg, SC: Reprint Company Publishers, n.d.

Seabrook, Lochlain. *Encyclopedia of the Battle of Franklin*. Franklin, TN: Sea Raven Press, 2012.

Sides, Hampton. *Blood and Thunder: An Epic of the American West.* New York: Doubleday, 2006.

Singletary, Otis A. *The Mexican War*. Chicago: University of Chicago Press, 1960.

Sword, Wiley. *Embrace an Angry Wind*. New York: HarperCollins Publishers, 1992.

———. *Shiloh: Bloody April.* Dayton, OH: Morningside Bookshop, 1988.

U.S. War Department. *The War of the Rebellion: A Compilation of the Official Records of the Union and Confederate Armies.* 128 vols. Washington, D.C.: Government Printing Office, 1900.

Utley, Robert Marshal. *Fort Union National Monument*. Washington, D.C.: United States Department of the Interior. Historical Handbook Number 35. National Park Historical Handbook. Series Number 35, 1962.

Warner, Ezra. *Generals in Gray.* Baton Rouge: Louisiana State University Press, 1991.

Warwick, Rick. *Williamson County: Civil War Veterans—Their Reunions and Photographs.* N.p.: Heritage Foundation of Franklin and Williamson County, 2007.

Watkins, Sam R. *Co. Aytch*. New York: MacMillan Publishing, 1962.

Waugh, John C. *The Class of 1846 from West Point to Appomattox: Stonewall Jackson, George McClellan and Their Brothers*. New York: Warner Books, 1994.

Wiley, Bell Irvin. *The Life of Johnny Reb: The Common Soldier of the Confederacy.* Baton Rouge: Louisiana State University Press, 1980.

Woodworth, Steven E. *Jefferson Davis and His Generals: The Failure of Confederate Command in the West.* Lawrence: University of Kansas Press, 1990.

Young, Kevin R. *To the Tyrants Never Yield: A Texas Civil War Sampler.* Plano, TX: Wordware Publishing Inc., 1992.

Unpublished

Adams, Rita Grace. "Biography of a Frontier American." PhD diss., St. Louis University, 1964. (Copy in possession of author.)

Adams, Thomas Patton. "Family History." N.d. (Unpublished manuscript, copy in possession of author.)

———. Letter to author, July 16, 1996. (Copy in possession of author.)

Carter House Collection. John Adams File, including article on Nathan Adams from "History of Davidson County" and diary of Confederate soldier. (Copies in possession of author.)

Clemmons, Ronald T. "Death of General John Adams." (Copy in possession of author.)

Cowles, Mary Ormond Adams collection. Obituary of Mrs. Martha Adams, January 15, 1854. (Copy in possession of author.)

Cox, Rosalie Adams. "Family History." 1960. (Copy in possession of author.)

Crawford, Jeanne Cloyes. "Adams and Eldridge Brief Sketches." Memphis, TN. (Copy in possession of author.)

Fraley, David. "Major General W.W. Loring's Confederate Division at the Battle of Franklin, Tennessee, November 30, 1864." 2002. (Copy in possession of author.)

———. "Notes on the Eastern Flank Deployment/Fighting During the Battle of Franklin, Tennessee 30 November, 1864." N.d. (Copy in possession of author.)

Friend, Louise Arnold, reference historian. Department of the Army, U.S. Army Military History Institute, Carlisle Barracks, Carlisle, PA. Letter to author. (Copy in possession of author.)

McDougall, Thomas Mower. "A Tribute to Charles McDougall and Marie Hanson McDougall." January 1, 1902. (Copy in possession of author.)

Sprague, Harry S. Clippings scrapbook, vol. 2, p. 167. (Copy in possession of author.)

St. Louis Society Scrapbook, 1889–1906, p. 26, "Three Weddings in St. Louis Society Celebrated Today." (Copy in possession of author.)

Internet

"American Memory: A History of Lawmaking for a New Nation Journal of the Confederate Congress, a Century of Lawmaking for a New Nation: U.S. Congressional Documents and Debates, 1774–1875." rs6.loc.gov/cgi-bin/query/D?hlaw:7:./temp/~ammem_DbL0 (accessed August 2014, site discontinued).

American Pacific Line. "Travel Times New York to San Francisco." www.apl.com/history/html/timeline_01.html#2 (accessed August 2014, site discontinued).

Ancestry.com. "History of Davidson County, Tennessee." freepages.history.rootsweb.ancestry.com/~nashvillearchives/willoughbyI.html (accessed March 5, 2010, site discontinued).

Ancestry.com, including Rootsweb, accessed by researcher Marsha Smith various dates, November 2016.

ArlingtonNationalCemetery.net. "Thomas Mower McDougall." www.arlingtoncemetery.net/tmmcdoug.htm (accessed November 2, 2016).

Army of the Cumberland and George Thomas. "The Spencer Rifle." www.aotc.net/Spencer.htm (accessed November 2, 2016).

BattleofFranklinTrust.com. "The Carter House History." www.battleoffranklintrust.org/carterhouse_history.htm (accessed November 8, 2016).

Blueandgrayeducation.org. "A Story in Warfighting: Nathan Bedford Forrest and the Battle of Brice's Crossroads." www.blueandgrayeducation.org/publications/monographs/a-study-in-warfighting (accessed December 3, 2016).

Buckhead Heritage Society. "Moore's Mill." www.buckheadheritage.com/sites/default/files/file/Battle%20of%20Moore's%20Mill%20Map%20and%20Orders.pdf (accessed October 2, 2013, site discontinued).

Byler, Edgar D., III. "General John Bell Hood's Invasion of Tennessee October 1864–January 1865: The Wayne County Tennessee Passage." www.tngenweb.org/wayne/Hood.htm (accessed December 3, 2016).

Civilwarartillery.com. "Basic Facts Concerning Artillery." www.civilwarartillery.com/basicfacts.htm (accessed November 5, 2016).

Civilwarhome.com. "Journal of the Army of Tennessee." www.civilwarhome.com/journalaotnashville.htm (accessed November 10, 2016).

CivilWarReference.com. "George Hollins." www.civilwarreference.com/people/index.php?peopleID=2092 (accessed October 3, 2013, site discontinued).

Cox, Debie. "Turnpikes and Bridges in Davidson County, Tennessee." Nashville History blog spot. nashvillehistory.blogspot.com/2014/07/turnpikes-and-bridges-in-davidson.html (accessed December 3, 2016).

Findagrave.com. "Georgiana McDougall Adams." www.findagrave.com/cgi-bin/fg.cgi?page=gr&GRid=45277855 (accessed November 3, 2016).

———. "Mary Margaret Adams." www.findagrave.com/cgi-bin/fg.cgi?page=gr&GSln=adams&GSfn=mary&GSmn=margaret&GSbyrel=all&GSdyrel=all&GSst=28&GScntry=4&GSob=n&GRid=35562521&df=all& (accessed December 4, 2016).

Firstladies.org. "First Lady Biography: Rachel Jackson." www.firstladies.org/biographies/firstladies.aspx?biography=7 (accessed December 3, 2016).

Fort Crook Historical Society. "Fort Crook Museum." www.fortcrook.com (accessed December 3, 2016).

Friends of Metropolitan Archives of Nashville and Davidson County. Ancestry.com. "Nashville Archives." freepages.history.rootsweb.ancestry.com/~nashvillearchives/willoughbyI.html (accessed 2010, site discontinued).

Gorenfeld, Will. "Battle of Santa Cruz de Rosales" and "Letter: Cave Couts to John Love." Musketoon.com. www.musketoon.com/2005/02/battle-of-santa-cruz-de-rosales-16.html (accessed October 29 and November 2, 2007, site discontinued).

Gulbransen, Ann Fox. Various entries related to Adams family history. GulbangiFiveFamilies.com. www.gulbangi.com/5families-o/p1.htm (accessed December 3, 2016).

Hardison, Dan. "St. John's Episcopal Church." The Episcopal Church and Visual Arts. ecva.org/congregations/features/st_johns_maury_county/st_johns_maurycounty.htm (accessed December 3, 2016).

HenryRifles.com. "Henry History." henryrepeating.com/henry-history.cfm (accessed December 3, 2016).

Hoss, Embree, and William B. Reese. "History of Nashville, Tennessee." Hackman-Adams.com. www.hackman-adams.com/guns/papermake.htm (accessed October 2, 2013, site discontinued).

Illinoisgenweb.org. "65th Illinois Infantry Regiment History." civilwar.illinoisgenweb.org/history/065.html (accessed December 3, 2016).

LancasteratWar.com. "The Battle of Sweeden's Cove, June 4, 1862." www.lancasteratwar.com/2012/06/skirmish-at-sweedens-cove-june-4-1862.html (accessed November 15, 2016).

Levasseur, Auguste. *Lafayette in America in 1824 and 1825*. Vol. 2. Philadelphia: Carey and Lea, 1829. Google Books, books.google.com (accessed December 3, 2016).

Mason, Jim. "Osage Orange." Great Plains Nature Center. www.gpnc.org/osage.htm (accessed December 3, 2016).

McWhorter, Samuel W. "Reyado." Ghosttowns.com. www.ghosttowns.com/states/nm/rayado.html (accessed December 3, 2016).

Mocivilwar150.com. "Missouri Civil War Sesquicentennial." mocivilwar150.com/history/battle/544 (accessed October 2, 2013, site discontinued).

Mustard, Karen. "Daring Deeds of Barry's Artillery." Genealogytrails.com. genealogytrails.com/tenn/hamilton/chattanoogasowndaringgdeedsofbarrysartillery.htm (accessed December 3, 2016).

National Park Service. "Dragoon Soldier." www.nps.gov/fosc/learn/education/dragoon-soldier.htm (accessed December 3, 2016).

———. "Fort Donelson." www.nps.gov/fodo/index.htm (accessed November 3, 2016).

———. "Places to Go in New Mexico." www.nps.gov/safe/planyourvisit/places-to-go-in-new-mexico.htm (accessed September 15, 2013, site discontinued).

Necaise, Nancy Somervell Nash. "James Knox Gibson Manuscript." Ancestry.com. freepages.genealogy.rootsweb.ancestry.com/~stantontnhistory/Civil_War.html (accessed December 3, 2016).

Nesbitt Memorial Library. "Diary of James T. Pettus." library.columbustexas.net/history/pettus%20diary.htm (accessed December 3, 2016).

Niepert, Robert. "Civil War Pontoon Bridges." Wadehamptoncamp.org. www.wadehamptoncamp.org/pontoon.html (accessed November 8, 2016).

Niu.edu. "Mechanicsburg Diary." dig.lib.niu.edu/ISHS/ishs-1963summer/ishs-1963summer-233.pdf (accessed October 10, 2013, site discontinued).

Pederson, Erica. "San Francisco History." www.sanfrancisco.com/history (accessed November 7, 2016).

San Diego Historical Society. "Cave Johnson Couts." www.sandiegohistory.org/bio/couts/couts.htm (accessed October 10, 2013, site discontinued).

———. "Rancho Guajome: An Architectural Legacy Preserved." *Journal of San Diego History* 41, no. 4 (Fall 1995). www.sandiegohistory.org/journal/95fall/guajome.htm (accessed June 6, 2005, site discontinued).

The State of Missouri Historical Society Famous Missourians. "Sterling Price." Shsmo.org. shs.umsystem.edu/historicmissourians/name/p/price (accessed November 8, 2016).

TerrysTexasRangers.org. "John Austin Wharton." terrystexasrangers.org/biographies/submitted/wharton.html (accessed January 10, 2007, site discontinued).

Texas State Historical Association. "Benjamin Lloyd Beall." www.tshaonline.org/handbook/online/articles/fbe04 (accessed August 3, 2013, site discontinued).

———. "John Austin Wharton." www.tsahaonline.org/search/node/john%20wharton (accessed August 15, 2014, site discontinued).

———. "William Harris Wharton." www.tshaonline.org/handbook/online/articles/fwh08 (accessed September 12, 2008, site discontinued).

To the Sound of the Guns. "24-Pdr Flank Howitzers." markerhunter.wordpress.com/2009/11/04/24-pdr-flank-howitzers (accessed November 8, 2016).

Union Pacific. "Significant Individuals," "General John Stephen 'Jack' Casement." www.up.com/aboutup/history/individuals/index.htm (accessed December 3, 2016).

USMA.edu (United States Military Academy). "A Brief History of West Point." www.usma.edu/wphistory/SitePages/Home.aspx (accessed November 10, 2016).

VisitMusicCity.com. "The Story of Music City." www.visitmusiccity.com/visitors/nashvillehistory (accessed November 8, 2016).

Waldren, Geoffrey R. "Death of Gen. Felix K. Zollicoffer." www.millsprings.net/index.php/2013-10-01-18-24-22/death-of-gen-felix-k-zollicoffer (accessed December 3, 2016).

WhiteHouse.gov. "James K. Polk." www.whitehouse.gov/about/presidents/JamesPolk (accessed November 8, 2016).

William L. Clements Library, Manuscripts Division, Finding Aids. University of Michigan. "John Love Papers." quod.lib.umich.edu/c/clementsmss/umich-wcl-M-3118lov?view=text (accessed December 3, 2016).

Index

A

About the Author

Bryan Lane and his family live in Spring Hill, Tennessee, less than one and a half miles from the Familiar Road. He has researched General Adams for more than twenty years, working with Adams's family members and visiting many of the sites mentioned in the book. His articles have been published by *Civil War Times Illustrated* and *Blue and Gray*. Bryan is an OSHA workplace safety consultant and trainer for the University of Tennessee.